THE SIMPLE MANIFESTO

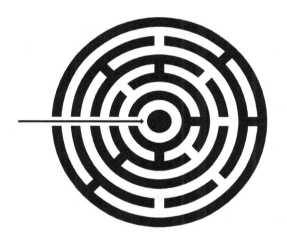

Marketing principles to save you time, increase profit and create your dream business in a SNAP!

WES TOWERS

Endorsements

The Simple Manifesto is strikingly innovative in its approach, stepping outside of the square to challenge its readers. Thought-provoking and insightful, Wes gives power to the reader by leaving any decisions in the reader's hands. *The Simple Manifesto* goes against all the rules in the best way possible, challenging everything you thought you knew about marketing. Really, a great read!

Pauline Rooney, MPC, NLP, HYP, Dip Y, Presenter, Author

Wes Towers has created a masterpiece. The title of the book speaks volumes because the book contains insights that are simple, yet very powerful when implemented. Wes guides you through a process on how to make your business more successful. This book is a must-have for you, the business owner.

Ronny Prasad, Author of *Welcome to Your Life – Simple insights for your inspiration and empowerment.*

I thoroughly enjoyed reading *The Simple Manifesto*. Fundamentally, our businesses, success and results in life all stem from who we are, what we believe, think, value and the actions we take. Our minds are the root of all things. I particularly enjoyed the first few chapters where Wes has drilled down on these fundamentals and poses questions which every business owner or aspiring business owner should take time to answer, even if they think they already know them. Reassessing what we do regularly, being open to new ideas and different ways of doing things, is critical to thrive in our fast paced changing world. Wes writes in a down to earth and engaging manner, which ensures his book is easy to read, entertaining and most important, useful.

Mandy Napier, Mind & Performance Coach, Published Author and Speaker

The Simple Manifesto is packed with practical advice to help small business owners market their products and services successfully. Each section has real life examples of what works, and what doesn't, plus searching questions to help you clarify and simplify your business.

John P Dawson, Managing Partner, Dawson McDonald Consulting

The Simple Manifesto is written in a clear understandable way for the reader who is not web-savvy but needs to be. I found the guides on networking, creating an elevator pitch, and writing blogs extremely helpful. And I even know now how SEO works! I used Wes' words to instruct my website designers so I sound like I know what I am talking about! I will certainly be following the checklist the next time I write a blog. I would recommend this book highly for any business owner who has expertise in their own industry, but is bewildered by marketing and how to promote themselves in the current environment.

Glenda May, International Leadership Facilitator, Certified Executive Coach & Author of the '*52 Ways*' Series

I have read hundreds of books on business over the years and after a while they all start to sound the same so when I read *The Simple Manifesto*, it was like a breath of fresh air. Written with simplicity in mind it took me through the process of viewing my business from a different angle. I could really relate to the stories and strategies throughout the book and with each chapter, new and exciting ideas started to appear (I filled an entire note pad). If you are looking for a book that will give you a fresh perspective on business this is it!

Amanda Robins, Superfy HQ, Intuitive Creative Director

For more endorsements and reviews visit:
www.simplemanifesto.com/testimonials/

First published in 2015 by Omnific Design

6/4 Techno Park Drive
Williamstown, Victoria 3016
Australia
www.omnificdesign.com.au

Author: Wes Towers

Title: The Simple Manifesto : Marketing principles to save you time, increase profit and create your dream business in a SNAP!

ISBN: 978-0-9943676-0-0

Subjects: Web sites, New Business Enterprises, success in business, small business, entrepreneurship, business planning

Cover design and internal design by Wes Towers
Book Coach & Preliminary Editor: Sheridan Morris
Editor: Alan Gilmour

Disclaimer

The material in this publication is of the nature of general comment only, and does not represent professional advice. It is not intended to provide specific guidance for particular circumstances and it should not be relied on as the basis for any decision to take action or not take action on any matter which it covers. Readers should obtain professional advice where appropriate, before making any such decision. To the maximum extent permitted by law, the author and publisher disclaim all responsibility and liability to any person, arising directly or indirectly from any person taking or not taking action based upon the information in this publication.

This book is dedicated to four of the greatest people on the planet.

Firstly my wife Lisa, who has made many sacrifices in her own life to allow me to build my business.

Secondly, to my awesome kids Max, Charlie and Grace. You are all amazing, unique and gifted.

I'm blessed to have you in my life.

Wes / Dad

Table of Contents

Foreword

Have you ever just snapped... not in a good way? Just totally lost your cool and wanted to break something?

One of my strongest (and possibly fondest) memories working alongside Wes Towers involved one of those moments. At the time, I was a few years into a publishing venture called Anthill Magazine. We'd commissioned Wes to manage the design. And, of course, we wanted every edition to be creative, exciting and jump from the newsstand.

But, like most young businesses, we weren't yet big on 'process'. And this meant that, more often than not, we would find ourselves working around the clock, engaged in a mad and unstructured flurry of activity to file our magazine on time.

On this particular occasion, Wes had joined us in the office to see if he could help us meet another looming deadline.

And things, for once, were working out. Whispers began to spread throughout the office, like a happy summer breeze, that we might actually get this edition filed at the time we were supposed to. We began to relax, crack jokes and even make dinner plans (an act strictly taboo on deadline).

Of course, we were tempting fate. And, before you could say, "Great job. That's a wrap," someone pressed the wrong button and we lost eight hours of design work. (Rather, we lost eight hours of Wes' design work.)

And Wes snapped.

But, to his credit, he did not shout. He did not stamp his feet. He did not start casting blame. Rather, he turned beetroot red and went for a walk. When he returned, maybe 20 minutes later, he settled back into the job and helped us get to where we needed to be.

Now, I don't tell this story to highlight the better points of Wes' unflappable temperament. (That's not why you are reading this book.) I tell this story as one of many 'muck ups' that took place in this particular business, Anthill Magazine, and as one of many mistakes that could have proven extremely damaging or even fatal...

...but didn't.

And, when you read this book, you will perhaps understand why. You see, setbacks are part and parcel of business. They happen in every commercial enterprise every day. Some are minor. And some are major.

What I often find strange, however, is how the same challenge in different businesses can have vastly different consequences. In the case of my magazine, there were many incidents that could have brought about our sudden demise, more than I care to remember.

Yet...

Investors continued to invest money, even after it was clear that print magazines were on the way out. Staff worked for salaries that were less than they could have earned elsewhere, despite having a boss who clearly had no understanding of 'process'. Customers continued to support the brand, even as we morphed into an on-line community in 2009, and then an educational product in 2014.

And guys like Wes gave us a second chance and didn't walk out, even when we were being unreasonable (or committing stupid, unintentional acts of self-sabotage).

It sometimes seems amazing that Anthill has lasted as long as it has, you could say 'despite the odds'.

But then again...

Despite our many failings, despite the GFC, despite my own lack of experience, despite the fact that most businesses don't make it past their third birthday, we survived... and, in time, we thrived.

And why is that? (Well, it wasn't because of intelligent management, in its early years, I can tell you that.)

Put simply, we always had four unmalleable principles to live by... even if we didn't know what to call them yet.

And they looked something like this:

- Standpoint

- Nonconformist

- Approach

- Position

You will notice, as you read on, that none of these words specifically reference what your business does, or even how you do it – at least not from a purely tactical standpoint.

They relate to something deeper, a mystery that you will unravel as you travel through the pages of this book.

They relate to foundational principles that help some organisations overcome challenges, win the support of stakeholders (perhaps even when they might not deserve it), and transform staff and customers into champions and advocates.

Because at the end of this 'Simple Manifesto', if you paid attention, if you follow the lessons within its pages, you too will be able to forge your own sustainable path, despite whatever mistakes and setbacks and obstacles the turbulent world of business might throw your way.

And, then, it will be your turn to SNAP... but in a good way.

by James Tuckerman

James Tuckerman is one of Australia's most accomplished digital publishers and the founder of numerous ventures to support new business, including Anthill Magazine, the Not-So-Freaky University, the SMART100, the 30UNDER30 and the Cool Company Awards.

What if the Business Gurus Were Wrong?

You get told you need complex marketing systems, elaborate sales pitches, social media "relationships", manuals, employee management systems, policies, procedures, org charts, pie charts, hierarchies...What if everything you have heard about small business was wrong?

The Simple Manifesto challenges conventional marketing strategies, with their prescriptive, step-by-step formulas that are hard to understand, and eat up your precious time implementing, despite costing a lot of money. You get told these conventional, complicated strategies work, and they can be great in theory, but you probably feel that they're not for you.

Small business owners and entrepreneurs in our fast-paced, ever-changing business environment don't need systems; they need simple. You don't need complicated; you want achievable, practical and helpful advice fast. Something to turn to for ideas, or when the going is tough. You want to know the common challenges facing people just like you, and see some ideas to overcome them – ideas that worked and ideas that didn't, so you can save time by not making the same mistakes. This book helps you throw away the complexity so you reach your big goals, efficiently and effectively. You may even enjoy yourself. The ideas are simple, fun, sometimes counterintuitive and maybe even controversial. Best of all, they're not complex and that's what you need.

The Crossroads

I started my business with a set of ideals and dreams of what it would mean to me, my family and the community around me: more money, more freedom and more time to invest into causes I felt were important. That was the dream. Lots of people start small businesses with a dream just like this but often it doesn't produce what they intended. You start off wanting to be an entrepreneur and end up somewhere else, not doing what you imagined. The facts show that this happens often. This book is written to change that.

Life throws up its fair share of challenges. These challenges often become pivotal times in our lives. They are times when we come to a crossroad and decisions are made that affect the course of our history.

I've come to many crossroads in my life, some through circumstances outside my control, others as a result of my own decisions. Some decisions turned out to be good, others have been terrible. The good news is, while decisions made at the crossroads can often feel permanent, most are flexible and reversible.

If you don't like the direction your business or life it taking, you can adapt, you can reshape things, you can improve. If your decision turns out to be holding you back from reaching your goal or your destiny, you can make a new decision and move on. This book will help you do just that, yet you'll call the shots. I'm not going to demand anything of you. I'm not going to tell you to follow my decisions, you will make your own.

I've learnt a lot the hard way – by trial and error. I've also learnt in the trenches, getting my hands dirty with hundreds of small and micro-businesses. I've been working in Marketing in one way, shape or form since February 2000 and I've learnt a lot from clients' successes and even more from their failures. I'd much prefer to learn from someone else's mistakes than make those mistakes myself! It's faster, cheaper and leaves me free to have fun with what I am doing.

My goal is to share the values and principles I've learnt from, and now live by while running my business. You may adopt these ideas. You may reject them. You may find some of them unconventional. However, I encourage you to face the challenge and make your own decisions. Your business becomes a reflection of yourself and will manifest your own values and principles, so the more you value what you are building, the better your business will be.

I came to the crossroads in my own journey when my conscience bailed me up, slapped me around a little, and asked some difficult questions.

Let me explain…

Introduction

It was 2:11am on a Friday morning in early December, 2005. I had a speaking engagement at a business breakfast meeting lined up, so on Thursday evening I dug out some old notes to rework into my presentation. Pretty soon, the creative juices kicked in and I was off dreaming, planning and exploring new ideas. I even plotted opportunities for my business in the New Year. Creative ideas feel pretty good and the flow of ideas was a lot of fun. The meeting preparation was forgotten about as I pressed on into the night.

Suddenly I realised that I would need to be up in just a few hours' time for the meeting. Still no meeting preparation. Realising sleep was more important than anything I could prepare now, I threw myself into bed. "Go to sleep, go to sleep, go to sleep," I looked at the clock and the breakfast meeting was even closer. "Quick. Go to sleep. Go to sleep." I started to get angry with myself; you can imagine how that worked. I crawled out of bed at 5.45am to face the day, with no great presentation to show for a sleepless night.

I fronted up to speak and rattled off the same old stuff I'd said many times before. Similar stuff to what I've heard all the platform speakers say. The audience seemed to soak it up. There were plenty of head nods and smiles. They enjoyed the message, and later on I enjoyed the backslaps over strong coffee.

By midday, I started to crash. The lack of sleep caught up with me, so I decided to take an early "beer-o'clock," go home and put my feet up. Laying back on the couch, I started to consider the message I shared in the morning. It was successful enough but it began to weigh heavily on me. Maybe it was the lack of sleep, but my conscience was really playing on me. I asked myself some serious questions:

"Do I actually believe in what I spoke about?"

"Does this stuff actually work in the real world?"

"Do I just rehash old ideas because they appeal to the audience?"

"Am I making a difference to people? Isn't that the point, rather than just getting through it? "

My values and principles were being challenged. People had wanted to know what I think and I had just regurgitated the same old messages. Even worse: other people's messages. I realised that just because all the gurus spruik the same ideas, doesn't make those ideas right. Where did it all come from in the first place? I realised it was time to challenge conventional wisdom and find out what actually works and what doesn't – for my own business and, in turn, the businesses I work with.

Renew your mind

In my sleep-deprived state I started with a question all the business gurus ask: Is your business working for you or are you working for your business?

Great question but how do you qualify that? There's a mindset issue to overcome first – the typical business model values busy-work. You know how it happens: as an employee, the busier you look, the more you're valued, the higher you climb the corporate ladder.

We get trained to look and stay busy. We brag about how busy we are. I attend networking events and the small talk is often, "Are you busy?" Almost always, the answer is, "Yes, flat out." People even boast about it: "I was so busy that I couldn't even…" I wonder if they're "busy" worrying where their next customer is coming from, how to pay the bills, or even their social media. I don't mean that to sound disrespectful to anyone, but I do wonder why we obsess about being busy. The truth is, it's a crazy question to ask small business owners who often earn a lot less than they would if they had a 'normal' day job, and are usually far busier.

Work ethic isn't the problem. I'll deal with the busy-work belief system later in this book. I've seen many common trends that send start-up and small business owners crazy and even cause many to fail. The problem is they are not spending their time and effort on the most effective work. They are the wrong kind of busy. This book shows it's time to transition from filling up each day with busy-work, to focus on what matters. You can achieve more while doing less and I'll show you how.

So who am I to write this book anyway?

If you have found yourself wondering this about me, congratulations! You should always ask this type of question no matter how popular or well-regarded the author is. Challenge everything and think independently.

As I've already said, I work with small businesses, start-ups and entrepreneurs. People who are trying to make a living from their dreams. People just like you. Most of my learning has been 'in the trenches', getting my hands dirty in the thick of things. The real world marketplace is the best place to learn and grow. There's nothing like taking on a job you are not quite sure how to do and figuring it out as you go. It seems to me that this is exactly how it happens for most small business owners.

Yes, I have got a degree, I gained a Bachelor of Visual Arts (Graphic Design/Multimedia) in 1999. That was fun but, like a lot of people, it was only when I got my first job in a boutique marketing company that I realised what I didn't know. Or, more importantly for this book, how fast I would have to learn.

We were a 'cutting edge' Marketing company in Mosman, Sydney, yet we only had one computer with an Internet connection and that was a good old dial-up modem. When we landed our first website project, the team pointed to me and said, "This is your job!" The old-timers didn't want to learn the new technology so, as the new guy, it fell to me. To their credit, they gave me plenty of time to fumble my way through website design and development until we successfully completed the project. This is how it has always been for me, learning on the job when the pressure is on

> *"You don't learn to walk by following rules. You learn by doing, and by falling over."*
> **– Richard Branson**

and mistakes really matter. From then on, my learning about websites and online marketing has continued while also doing graphic design projects. Don't get me wrong, I still don't think I've 'arrived' as a website developer and marketer, or that I ever will. The learning will never end given the ever-changing nature of the Internet and that's just the way I like it!

This book is not a magic-bullet!

You may want a 'fix all', magic-bullet system. Something that will transform your business overnight into the successful company you've dreamt of.

The demand for this 'one size fits all' solution has led to thousands of programs, systems, DVDs, home-study courses and other educational products. As I've already said, I listen to this stuff too and do get some value from it. These programs usually have very attractive promises and guarantees, but they also carry the clause that you must follow the system EXACTLY as it's prescribed.

The problem is, what's prescribed is incredibly time-consuming or costly and therefore unachievable for most small business owners and entrepreneurs. For this reason, these step-by-step, how-to-do-it systems don't work. This is not a lofty, idealistic book. It's based on what I have observed in many businesses and what I've learnt in my own business.

This book is about creating options and flexibility in your business. It is my hope that you will find the inspiration, explanations and information you need to move forward in your business and achieve those big "gonna-do-it-one-day" goals you desire.

Be Selective

Entrepreneurial people typically have an abundance of ideas. Many of the ideas are fantastic and could be powerful if they were to implement them. The problem occurs when they don't focus their energies on one end goal. There is always a temptation to try the "next big thing" before completing what you had set out to do. You end up with stacks of half-done good ideas that produce mediocre results.

It is my fear that you will read this book in its entirety and then try to implement all the strategies all at once. Please don't do that! In fact, please do not read any further until you have read, understood, and absorbed, the first few chapters. Make this your filter by which all the tips, hacks and principles are understood.

"I like to turn things upside down, to watch pictures and situations from another perspective."
– Ursus Wehrli

By always chasing the "next big thing" and not focusing their energies on one main end goal, many business owners complicate the process. When you focus on the end goal, you can save time, reach your goals faster, and maximise your results without extra effort. In fact, you may reduce the required effort because you are so focused.

Pick and choose! The information in common business resources is usually great and the promises of what you can achieve by applying them may be true. The problem is, the time it takes to do all of it. Put a few of these systems together and you have an impossible, overwhelming task. The Simple Manifesto looks at these systems and programs differently and asks, "What of all this can I apply right now to what I already have, that is likely to create momentum?"

SNAP

You will find this book divided into four sections or lenses. I prefer to use the term lenses since each of the four highlights a fresh perspective on similar ideas and business principles. By defining these perspectives we simplify the business building process and create greater clarity for you, the leader and entrepreneur.

Each lens will help you view your business from a different angle. You will find ideas in this book intersect and intertwine frequently to create a complete picture. Some lenses will be more relevant for you to focus on right now and others may be more appropriate to consider further into your business journey or ignored completely. I encourage you to read the whole book and then choose to focus on the lens you feel will bring you the greatest impact right now.

The four lenses are: Standpoint, Nonconformist, Approach and Position... or SNAP for short. SNAP is the methodology behind The Simple Manifesto. It's the ideology behind the principles shared.

Lenses one and two are about your mindset as a business owner and entrepreneur. I'd suggest reading them away from your usual work environment. We want to break the patterns of your normal, day-to-day thinking and get creative. Go to the beach or another place you relax and enjoy so you can feel refreshed and be in a contemplative, creative state.

Lenses three and four are where we get our hands dirty and get stuff done. They are jam-packed with tips, tricks, principles, and advice, building on the foundations you create in lenses one and two. I suggest you read this with your laptop handy so you can take action on the fly. It's all part of a simple process. You'll need to get selective and decide what to implement now, what to consider later, and what to ignore completely. For example, if you are a brand new business, you may want to focus on the logo design chapter first. Once that's done you'll want to move on to your next steps. We will build your business together while avoiding the mistakes I've learnt from.

So that you can begin to grasp the concepts in each lens further, here's a quick overview.

Standpoint

This is your unique perspective. It's about your passion. It's about what makes you tick. While others foolishly disconnect their business from their personal values, it's the intersection of these two aspects of your life that create the most meaning and purpose. Your unique standpoint is how you view the world and what's important to you. It's based on your values and the past experiences that have shaped you. Your standpoint is what motivates you and creates your convictions. It's what will see you through good times and bad for the long term. It is difficult to be self-analytical and reflective while dealing with work pressure, so get out of your usual work environment while you read this lens.

Nonconformist

There's a little rebel inside all of us and that's not a bad thing. It's probably the reason why you started your own business and are reading this book. Nonconformity comes from your unique standpoint and it's what makes you interesting and compelling. It's likely there are aspects of your industry you cannot stand and believe there is a better way. There's stuff you believe in whole-heartedly that the majority passionately disagree with. This lens is about letting your competitors maintain the status-quo while you deliberately adopt a different approach. We will cover the benefits and challenges of the nonconformist business so you can make it work to your advantage.

Approach

It's about movement. It's about momentum. Yes you'll have setbacks and get off track at times, so it's a matter of adjusting your approach as you move forward. While previous lenses covered your mindset and beliefs, this is where we take action and begin to move toward our goals. I will uncover simple ideas and principles that will equip you to make progress faster than most believe is possible. It's about the journey of continuous improvement, not the destination.

Position

This is about your rock-solid position. The things you will not budge on based on the three preceeding lenses. We will explore ways to position your business by communicating your unique message to the right people. It's about positioning yourself and your business so your prospects 'get it'.

As a complete picture, SNAP represents a moment in time when change occurs. SNAP happens in times of triumph, but it also happens in moments of pain. As business owners and entrepreneurs, we all find ourselves on the mountaintops and, at other times, in the valleys. Breakdown is often just a few short steps from breakthrough. That's SNAP. It's not about starting again or a more wheel-spinning endeavour. Willpower, determination, and trying harder will only get you so far. It's when the existing components of your business and life realign in a new, clearly defined way to produce a better outcome. I don't know your story and I don't know how long you have been on the journey you find yourself on today. However I do know change can happen quickly when we simplify. Far quicker than most people think possible. I'll share some of my story (the good, the bad and the ugly) and also some from the people I know. I encourage you to relate these stories back to your own unique journey.

You're a business owner right? Ever been told by well-meaning friends and family to "snap out of it"? This book proposes it's time to SNAP into it. Let's get started.

standpoint

Noun:

An attitude to a particular issue.

Synonyms:

Point of view, viewpoint, vantage point, attitude, stance, stand, view, opinion, position, way of thinking, frame of mind, outlook, perspective, angle, slant

(Credit Google.com - edited)

In this lens I'll show you how to better define and establish your standpoint so it becomes the foundation for your business... but first let's look at the standpoint of this book and what it contains. At first, this may seem like an extention of the introduction (which it is) however, the hidden meaning will begin to emerge the deeper we go. A framework your own venture can be modelled on will be revealed as the pieces of the puzzle come together.

Why The Simple Manifesto?

We are living in a fast-paced, complex world where we are constantly bombarded with new messages, new information, new systems, new tools... the list goes on. While the new "stuff" is pitched to us in a way that highlights all the benefits of the new shiny thing, often times it adds complexity to our lives and restricts simplicity.

We are searching for simplicity – for an easier way of life. We dream of a tree or sea-change. We dream of working less and earning more so we can spend more time with our family or friends. We dream of retirement when we can do what we want, when we want. Whatever it is that excites and motivates you, you can start to experience now.

Many entrepreneurial people choose to start a business for the freedom it can provide – only to find they are free to work whatever 80 hours a week they like! Instead of them owning a business, the business owns them. Busy-ness is the enemy of business. Let's wage war against your enemy. People talk about busy-ness like it's something to boast about. They brag how busy they are. What if you challenged this conventional thinking? What if you reversed the order? What if you turned it inside out, upside down? What would it mean to your business and personal life?

Let me challenge you right now. Most of us have read multiple 'best-selling' business books yet, statistically, few of us apply what we learn. You can accept or reject my ideas and principles. However, they won't make a bit of difference in your business unless you do something about it. You may choose to reject everything I say. You may believe pursuing complexity is the best way forward for your business. That's fine! Do something about it. Let your passionate rejection of what I'm saying propel you forward.

I'm going to presume most readers will believe in the ideas and principles of this book. Chances are, if you picked up this book you are a creative thinker full of ideas and possibilities. You may not be short on great ideas but getting them all done is the challenge. It's a battle for many entrepreneurs. It is my intention to stir up more and more thoughts and ideas as you read on. Don't let this overwhelm you. Stay focused on whatever you are working on at the time. I'm not suggesting that you ignore new ideas. It's not possible or encouraged to shut down your creativity. Instead, create a brain dump for yourself. It can be as low-tech, or as high-tech as you like. It does not matter. Jot down any new thoughts and ideas you have so they are available for you later, but don't consume your thinking right now.

Sit on your ideas for a while and the best of them will continue to resurface. When it feels like the idea has you more than you have an idea, it's a good sign that it's something worth pursuing.

It's time to leave your comfort zone. It's like a swimming pool. You may be reluctant to jump right in, despite multiple people reassuring you that 'the water's beautiful'. However, once you take the courage to step in, you acclimatise and soon start to enjoy the pool. You forget your initial hesitation and begin to tell others that 'the water's beautiful'. Let me reassure you, the water is beautiful, so let's jump right in!

If your business is already in progress, implementing a completely new system will not be the best investment of your time and resources. This book is designed for you. If you're starting out, you probably need quick cash flow that can sustain you while you make further improvements. This book is also for you. It doesn't recommend implementing new systems that are going to cost massive amounts of time or money. It's about looking for small tweaks that take up minimal time but can be leveraged for maximum impact, fast.

We are not going to look at stories and case-studies from large corporations that you, as a small business leader or entrepreneur can't replicate. We won't be talking about how Nike, Virgin, Apple, or any other super successful company, run their business. I enjoy reading about and learning from these companies, however I also understand they are usually exceptional cases, and not what the majority of businesses can expect to experience by following a particular philosophy. We will be looking at unconventional ideas and new methods to create your own ideal business and lifestyle.

This book is not a 'rags-to-riches' story about how one guy started his business in his garage with $20 in his pocket and a credit card debt of thousands and turned his life around with a new idea or system that you too can implement. While I don't doubt that these stories happen, they are exceptional. There are many more stories of people in similar situations who failed miserably. They just don't write books! Like many people, I enjoy reading success stories. However we can't use them as a reliable model to run our own businesses.

This book provides an unconventional way of thinking, a method to experience frequent, incremental improvement. A way to minimise your time investment and maximise your profitability while doing what you love. There are three key principles every single strategy in this book should be measured by.

- Will this save me time?

- Will this increase my profit?

- Will this help create my dream business?

Keep these questions in the front of your mind, ahead of any strategy. They will help you quickly eliminate tasks from your to-do list that keep you trapped in the busy-work mindset.

These questions are universal yet the reasons why they are important will be unique to you and your values. You may want to make more money so you can support charities you are passionate about. Maybe you want to work fewer hours so you can spend more time with your family. Whatever you enjoy doing and are most passionate about will create the most meaning and purpose in your life – that's your dream business.

All of the ideas and principles in this book are created with the three questions in mind. However that doesn't mean you have to implement all of them in your business. It will depend on the state of your business right now. You have to make a judgment call on what needs your attention. Look for the low hanging fruit ready for you to pick. There is no 'one size fits all'. What you're looking for are the simple actions that won't take long to implement, produce profit fast, and give you a sense of personal satisfaction.

The Simple Agents (SAs)

Simple Agents (SAs) exist all around us – in every industry, in every city around the world. They choose not to be defined or governed by conventional thinking. We all know the kind of thinking that funnels people through universities to 'cubicle life', on to management and to leadership only by working harder and investing more and more time and effort. Until one day, at the end of their lives or on their death bed, they have an epiphany. It wasn't worth it! They wish they could turn back the clock, spend more time with loved ones, and more time doing what they love. SAs heed the warnings of those who have gone before them. They realise the time to live the life they dream of – is now. They see that they can start to live their best years immediately. These are 'the good old days', you're living them right now. This book will show you how to beat the system, remove the clutter and complexity in your life, and live on purpose. To design the life you desire and create a business to sustain that lifestyle sooner rather than later, get started NOW!

Not everyone is capable of becoming an SA. Some are far too brain-washed and indoctrinated by the system and can never break out of it. From the time they went to school, those in authority squeezed the uniqueness and creativity out of them. As the years passed by, they became more and more robotic – believing the same standpoints as everyone else, doing the same tasks as everyone else, and enjoying the same activities as everyone else. Thankfully not everyone was beaten down by the system to this mediocre existence. There are those who march to the beat of a different drum: the SAs.

SAs tend to be intuitive leaders with a strong sense of personal values. They are inspirational, motivational 'people's people'. They are enthusiastic, optimistic entrepreneurs filled with limitless potential. They are passionate and excited about their ideas, ideals, options and possibilities. Their passion is contagious as others adopt their unique standpoint. For SAs their satisfaction doesn't come from their product or service, but from the reason why they do what they do and why it's important to them.

They are creative people who are never content with the status-quo. They always believe there is a better, more exciting way to adapt their businesses. While they often have a broad range of skills and experiences, they see the bigger picture clearer than others. They don't allow themselves to be bogged down with minor details that can be delegated to someone else. They're unconventional thinkers and not afraid to try something new. They constantly search for fresh, more thrilling ways to challenge the industries they work in.

Onlookers at a distance sometimes believe they take too many risks, and seem inconsistent or without direction. They're wrong! SAs have a highly-tuned value system and standpoint by which they are guided. They care for people and want to create a better experience for clients, customers, and the people they work with. The SA sees what the future could be like before others can perceive it. They don't allow themselves to become restricted by formulas and processes that are not necessarily the best options. The SA is always prepared to try something different.

Some consider SAs to be too intense or extreme in their standpoint. This never stops them. The SA knows that their dream is still possible and achievable no matter what the knockers say. For SAs, there is a meaning behind their business that is more important than making money. However, they understand that the more money they make, the more they can invest back into whatever they're passionate about.

You won't find SAs working late into the night every day of the week at the expense of their families or personal lives. They find simple ways to produce the results they're looking for. Certainly, there will be times when they might work late, but it's because they're passionate about their business, not because they're just trying to 'keep their head above water'.

They particularly love the human interaction in business, yet at the same time thrive when they're able to spend time alone, dreaming of new, exciting opportunities and potential. Observers may mistakenly accuse them of doing 'nothing' during these quiet times; however it's at these times they become centred and able to harness the passion for the next venture.

I don't think we spend enough time in silence, just realising what's floating around in our noggin.
– Sandra Bullock

Flexibility is an advantage to SAs. They are fast starters, looking to gain momentum that can be adjusted and redirected as they progress. Because of their outward focus and people skills, they are often well liked and attract great people to work with them who will commit for the long term. They bring out the best in people and gather team players, who take care of the mundane, everyday tasks thereby allowing the SA to focus on the bigger picture. Later in the book, we will look at how even a micro-business can build a successful team of people to help it stay focused.

The SA doesn't allow their industry to control them, or dictate to them how business should be done. Some people might consider them rebels; however they don't tend to fight with people. They fight the system… and this book will show you how they win!

SAs often get into business for themselves because they can't find a fulfilling career path that is meaningful and interesting. They are restless explorers of possibilities, who don't want the 9 to 5 drudgery. They know the system can't support them or 'fix' them. They want to make a meaningful business based on their personal values and won't settle for anything less. These attitudes make the SA the perfect entrepreneur. Don't get me wrong, there's nothing wrong with the regular, working day until you retire – someone's got to do it, but it won't be an SA!

Does any of this sound like you?

Some readers of this book will relate closely to the SA. You will get a lot of value out of it as a result. Others may not relate at all with the SA and that's fine. If you are prepared to be challenged by new concepts and values, you too will find great value in reading this book.

The first thing to realise is that your most valuable asset is your time. You can generate more money and you can get more stuff that you feel is important, but you can't enjoy any of it if you don't have the time. We all get the same deal: 24 hours a day, 7 days a week. Your personal enjoyment and satisfaction are determined by how you spend this allocation of time.

Becoming an SA involves taking risks. The risks may be calculated, but even so, they remain risks. By running your business in a different way to your competitors you risk things not working out as you planned, looking like a fool, and being criticised by friends. Get over it! By making small tweaks and adjustments rather than big changes all at once, you will be taking mini-risks. Mini-risks are never fatal and are usually quickly reversible.

You'll find taking mini-risks gets easier as you make progress and build momentum. Whether it's with a new audacious marketing campaign, a website redesign, or the launch of a new innovative product, work out a way to break it down into small steps so they become mini-risks and minimise potential problems if they don't work out for you.

On this journey I will always encourage you to remain rock solid in your standpoint and the long-term vision of your business. However, I challenge you to remain flexible in the strategies and tactics you choose to implement to move forward. New opportunities present themselves regularly, so remain flexible to make the most of them. Flexibility is one area in which you can almost always beat the large corporations. They are far too big, slow, and clumsy, to respond quickly to new opportunities.

It's time to rediscover your passion and purpose so you can define your unique standpoint. If you're looking for meaning and purpose in your life it's unlikely you'll find it working a regular job. It may be possible if you work for a charity that you believe in, however the pay will likely be terrible so other areas of your life may suffer. When you run your own business, you call the shots. You decide what should be done. While it's not just about making more money, increased income is a handy bi-product of following your passion.

The Creativity Thief

We are all born with enormous creative potential. Many of us lose this creativity as we progress though life. We are taught to become more "realistic", more "down-to-earth", or more "predictable". While there is some merit in these attributes, they should never be embraced at the expense of your creativity.

As a child you probably day-dreamed frequently about what you were going to do and who you were going to become. Slowly but surely, the system attempted to squeeze this out of you. The busy-ness of life and increasing responsibilities of adult life made you feel trapped.

"Creativity takes courage."

– Henri Matisse

Don't worry! What was in you as a child still exists. What you dreamt about can be rekindled. It may possibly be expressed a little differently now, but that creativity inside you that makes you who you are is still alive and well. It's time to imagine again – to re-imagine where your life is headed and create your own future.

As a child you may have had great instincts and intuitively understood new concepts. These characteristics will be stirred up within you as you read this book. If you're not sure where to take your business, ask yourself, "What excited me as a child? What did I want to be before people told me that was silly? What would I become if nothing was impossible?"

Back when you were a child it was easy to imagine. It may take a little effort to get back into the habit but it is well worth it. Try activities you once did as a child, listen to music, or watch movies you loved. What was it that was important to you? Take back what's been stolen from you! Start dreaming again.

Don't let the fear of failure stop you. All of us fear something. It's a natural response to a potentially dangerous situation. It can be scary launching a new business or making changes in an established one. Stepping out of your comfort zone can be challenging. Don't let that stop you. Redefine the fear as excitement. Make the fear of not making the most of your opportunities greater than the fear of failure.

You may fear making the wrong decision, or fear being labelled a failure, or fear disappointing the people around you. It's a huge challenge for SAs who want to break the mould. The people around you are probably well meaning. They want you to get a reliable, secure job. They want you to take a long-term career path, maybe become a lawyer, a doctor, or whatever they perceive to be a good career path. It's a miserable life always trying to meet other people's expectations. Stop it now and live the life of your dreams. Even if it doesn't go according to plan, at least you won't die wondering.

Get people around you who can support you and mentor you. They need to believe in your unique standpoint. Get started as soon as you can. Even if it's baby steps, as you take action you will eliminate procrastination, and create momentum. It will become easier and you will pick up helpful feedback along the way so you can adjust or improve as you go.

Parties of Many, Parties of One

Learn to cope with, no, to enjoy, the spotlight. If you create anything meaningful it will attract attention. If you create something really meaningful, you will get a whole lot of attention. Some may be positive and some negative, and that's fine. You will rub shoulders with many people, some of whom you may not like. This applies to your time spent online, with your business partners, and with your customers.

SAs understand the importance of relationships so they become great networkers. They enjoy helping others. With this selfless approach they attract reciprocity. They build strategic alliances and friendships with like-minded people so everyone benefits. They are people's people, either naturally or as a learnt skill. They network at events, social gatherings, and on social media. They have a clearly defined standpoint, and an interesting perspective and story to tell.

The old, bland elevator pitch will never cut it, as we will explore later in this book. It's not a performance, SAs engage with excitement and passion instinctively. They can't contain their passion – It oozes out of them. It's not about personality types either. Extroverts and introverts will both communicate their passion in their own unique way. They can't help it. They have something they believe to be valuable and interesting to share. They enjoy the party!

It's also valuable for SAs to withdraw from the crowd. To shut out the noise. To spend time alone dreaming and thinking of new, exciting adventures such as creating a business. If you spend all your time with others, you will slowly become like them. The mob will convince you with their reasoning why life is the way it is. It sounds logical and reasonable, but the trouble is it creates drones. It builds the status-quo that you must try to avoid. By all means consider the ideas they present. Mull over them in your own quiet time, then look at the ideas from the opposing view.

What would it look like if you did business or lived life differently to the crowd? What would happen? What would it mean? While there's probably good reason why the mob follows one set of ideas, there may be equally good reasons to live by a different set. While there are no guarantees it will work, you are guaranteed to be unique – and unique often works far better than being 'one of the crowd'. Spend some time alone and consider opposing views to the norm. Do whatever works for you – go for a walk, go to the beach, climb a mountain, or listen to some music. Whatever it is that you enjoy and gives you time alone to think. Enjoy a party of one!

What I Learnt from an Ice Addict

I've known Jack for over 10 years and consider him a friend. He and his wife, Chloe, are a similar age to my wife, Lisa, and I. We had our first kids around the same time. They certainly had different backgrounds than we did but, overall, we had a lot in common as life stood at that time, even if they had done it a bit rough. Similar interests, a similar sense of humour and similar lives made us close. Unfortunately for Jack and Chloe, challenging times hit.

After the suicide death of an extended family member, they were forced to take care of a young relative. She was a troubled girl coming out of a dysfunctional home. Despite Jack and Chloe's best efforts, the additional responsibilities on top of their own young family became too much. There seemed to be no relief from the pressure so they turned back to the habits of their younger years – they turned to drugs. I don't pretend to understand addiction completely and I don't want to sound critical or judgmental about Jack and Chloe, I love them both. However there are many lessons I've learnt from watching how their standpoints were formed.

It seems to me that addictions are habits amplified to such a point that they control your actions. While drugs provide temporary relief and take the burdens and stress away, they eventually get a grip of your entire life and control you. All you want is the next hit, the next piece of temporary relief from the pain of life. Jack distanced himself from us, probably ashamed of his choices, until one day Lisa and I saw him walking on the street. He no longer looked like the Jack we knew. He looked like a homeless old man. You could see he was bitter and hardened. The kind of person you would usually try to avoid on the street. We stopped our car and ran over to him, wanting to see how he was and if we could help him in some way. He was happy to see us but told us of his troubled existence. He told us he wasn't the same person anymore. He had broken up

> *"The final forming of a person's character lies in their own hands."*
> **– Anne Frank**

with Chloe and their son was living with his grandparents. He had lost his family home and was living on the streets with nothing but a few bags of old clothes and blankets. How did Jack end up where he was? I guess there are lots of reasons and I'm sure he would have a different perspective than I do. Here's what I could see had happened to him and it's surprisingly relevant for those of us who run businesses.

Addiction binds your mind. Jack has a negative mindset that seems to grow increasingly worse. It's like a self-fulfilling prophecy. It's remarkable how we tend to move toward that which we focus on. That's why it's so important to get your standpoint right, it determines your perspective. Jack expects the worst in people and that's often what he experiences. He lives on the street, or squats in unoccupied homes or warehouses until he is moved on. On one occasion he woke to a loud noise. They were demolishing the house with him still inside. I've taken my two boys to see Jack in some of the places he has lived in. Their little hearts break for him but it's important to show them how to love people who others would reject. They also get to see first-hand what drugs and poor decisions can do. Jack's poor decisions have almost always come from a poor standpoint. The standpoint of hopelessness led to the drug taking. The standpoint of mistrust stops him from getting help from people. The standpoint of blaming Chloe prevents him from taking responsibility and making changes. It's a terrible cycle and one I've not been able to help him break.

While you may not be in the same situation as Jack, we all have standpoints based on incorrect assumptions that limit us and prevent us from breaking through and taking our businesses and lives to the next level. We often hold on to incorrect assumptions and they dictate how we run our businesses. These assumptions are what control us and we find ways to support them so they too become self-fulfilling prophecies. It becomes a cycle we find hard to break out of. It takes a positive mindset to create a great business. It takes a new perspective, a life-altering moment when you decide to question the status-quo and look for new ways to produce better results.

You will experience a number of breakthroughs in your life and in your business which will cause you to step out, break the rules, and create your own unique lifestyle. The biggest breakthrough is getting started. Making a decision to launch a new business and actually doing it are two different things. Start as soon as you can and start as small as you can. While your enterprise is still small it's a great time to experiment with your ideas as you develop your business. It's all part of the process of creating your own simple, repeatable, scalable marketing system.

If you have already started, congratulations! You're on the journey to escape the mundane life of the corporate world. Why would you want to act like them ever again? Enjoy the freedom and have fun. You call the shots. Every business is different. What's most important to your business may be completely different for others. Decide ahead of time what breakthroughs you want to achieve. As you go through this book you will probably have a number of creative ideas. It is only when these ideas are activated that they become powerful.

You don't need to do everything yourself either. Don't get overwhelmed. Break it down into bite-sized chucks and ignore the rest. You can reconsider your choices later but don't let that distract you right now. You may be faced with challenges and obstacles. Take the lessons learnt in these times and keep the passion for your dream alive.

The Standpoint Shift

Creativity should be the lens through which you view the world, no matter what you do. It is how you shape your unique standpoint. If you're going to create an unconventional business, play by your own rules, work less and earn more, it's going to take creative thinking to get you there. The biggest killer of creativity is a lack of confidence.

Most of us have our doubters, those people who don't believe we can make it happen, those who don't think we should take risks. Get past all this negativity and take action. Don't let negativity hold you back. Creating the business of your dreams requires confidence. Have faith that your ideas will work.

Confidence manifests itself not only in the way you see yourself and the actions you take, but also in the way others see you. When you lack confidence, others can see it. Maybe you're fearful of stepping out of your comfort zone. Maybe you are fearful of using a new, daring business model. When you don't believe in yourself, nobody else will either.

> *"When I was about ten, I was very impressed by the way Tarzan could swing through the trees from vine to vine. No one ever told me, 'Don't try this at home.'"*
> **– James Dobson**

Obstacles happen. The only way to avoid obstacles is to become stagnant! There are no such thing as obstacles if you're not trying to go somewhere.

While many people may be comfortable with a stagnant kind of lifestyle, SAs thrive on continuous personal and business development. Find a way to get past your fears. Ultimately you need to be clear in your standpoint when obstacles do occur.

Approach your business from a different angle. Sometimes we are too close to our businesses and cannot easily identify the best way forward.

Often the breakthrough comes when we step away from the situation and look for new ideas. Look outside your usual influences and see what you can adapt by taking a fresh perspective. Look across other industries to see how other entrepreneurs approach business.

Try not to do everything on your own. Brainstorm with other creative minds. Sometimes an external perspective helps. Give them permission to speak openly, even ruthlessly, and bite your tongue if you don't agree. Never blindly follow someone else's opinion. Try to understand the opinion givers so you can better define your own beliefs in a more compelling way.

The more you experience, the more awareness, presence, intuition and capacity you develop. Most of us believe in learning from our mistakes. Some go as far as saying you should fail fast and fail often to speed up the learning process. They have a point but, whenever possible, I'd rather learn from the failures of others than go through the pain of it myself. I'm not trying to fail fast or often, thank you!

To streamline the learning process, learn from others who have 'been there, done that' and learnt the hard way. Your situation won't be an exact match to theirs, however similar patterns and principles are likely to exist. You can also learn from unconventional, seemingly unrelated industries and communities. Patterns and principles often exist across many aspects of life. By viewing your business from a completely different angle, you will be better placed to create something unique and compelling.

A New Sales Standpoint

Over the years I've worked with a number of people looking to grow their businesses. What they want is marketing to produce sales, yet many are not very happy about 'selling'. It's an unhealthy standpoint that is based on our assumption of what sales is, and what sales people are like. Don't let this standpoint control your decisions. We have all experienced pushy, slimy sales people that we can't trust. That's exactly what we don't want to be seen as. You don't want to be like this, and you shouldn't need to if your business is built on a solid foundation. By changing our understanding of what selling is about, we'll be more comfortable and confident about it and won't self-sabotage our success.

Sales is about relationships. Build relationships with customers and care for them, and their needs, as people. Often a sale is the result of the relationship, not the product or service you sell. If you focus on relationship building, you will create loyalty. While this may not produce the quick profit that a purely money-driven strategy might, long-term you will build a loyal customer base of repeat buyers. Even if what you supply is unique, there are often comparable solutions that fulfil the same customer needs. If you focus purely on selling your product or service, you may end up falling into the trap of competing on price alone. If you have a strong relationship, you compete based on who you are.

> *"I don't want to say work is who I am, but some people feel more centred and more whole when they're producing and creating."*
> **– Ray Romano**

When you genuinely care for your customers, you will only ever sell what you believe to be a fantastic solution for them. We are all sick of sales people who try and sell us the highest ticket item trying to make a quick buck. I recall many times when I have advised customers not to take a particular service from us because I felt it wasn't the best fit for their business, even though it would have produced a quick profit for us. Often a lower-cost option will produce an equally good, if not better result.

Let me make a confession. An example from the early days of running my business that I'm now embarrassed about. I was asked to quote on a custom-created website and online system for a new business. The prospect sent me his business plan and how he intended the website to function. At the time I felt is was a poor business idea and I knew it wouldn't work. I convinced myself it was okay to go ahead with the project because it was his decision. I sent in my proposal and won the job. We completed the work and launched the website. It all looked great and worked great, however there was no market for it. Nobody cared. That business still has not produced one sale. If I had my time again, I would have advised the customer of ways they could test their business concept before investing thousands of dollars into a website. There are always ways to test your assumptions so you can see if a business idea is viable. Yes, the project produced a profit for us and it wasn't really my fault it didn't work because we followed the brief perfectly. However, I still feel I should have handled the situation better.

It's good to have ambition and a desire to sell, provided you are selling what you believe in. Belief gives you self-confidence, and self-confidence creates believability when selling. It's difficult to be confident if you don't believe passionately in your business. The same goes for employees too. If your team doesn't believe in your business they will find it hard to sell it. These days most people see straight through a slick salesperson, but will pick up on, and engage with, a genuinely passionate one.

Dream Settings

Most leaders agree, setting long-term goals is one of the keys to achieving success. Something amazing happens in your sub-conscious when you set goals. It often helps to redefine goals by using the word dreams. Dreams are exciting, passionate, and motivating, whereas goals can be about cold hard facts and figures that don't always inspire us to move forward.

To motivate yourself, define the reasons why you want to achieve your dreams. You need a strong reason why your business exists. Of course it's to live the lifestyle you desire, but there is probably something deeper than that. It could be to support a cause you believe in, or the satisfaction of problem solving to serve your customers in a better, more meaningful way.

Remaining motivated and enthusiastic about your business becomes contagious. If you love your business, you'll be fanatical about your products and services, which rubs off on the people around you. We often hear about people who made 'quick' money in a business. We hear their stories because they are rare and interesting, but the reality is, most business success is built incrementally over time. It's about finding out what the next step is that will edge you closer to your dreams. We will cover this in detail in Lens 3.

Your dreams help you define your standpoint. Without this focus it is difficult for you and your team to remain committed to the journey. Your mind uses pictures and words to seek out solutions for what it is searching for. See yourself being successful and anticipate positive results. For your team, communicate your standpoint so they take hold of it for themselves. There is a transference of enthusiasm when your team buys into your dreams. If you are not enthusiastic about your business, your customers and team members won't be either.

"When a person starts to talk about their dreams, it's as if something bubbles up from within. Their eyes brighten, their face glows, and you can feel the excitement in their words."

– John C. Maxwell

When you believe in your dream, you will be prepared to pay for success in advance. You'll keep yourself motivated and that rubs off on the people you influence. You set the tone in your business. Confidently expect to succeed. Make your self-fulfilling prophecy a positive one. Take responsibility for any failures and find ways to turn them into greater success. If you are already in business and don't love what you do, stop right now before you burn yourself out. It might be that you need to reconsider the kind of business you are in, or redefine what you do, so it's a better fit for your personality.

Keep on reviewing your processes. What did you do well? What would you do differently next time? How can you tweak your approach to move closer to your dreams? Focus on what you are doing well and celebrate the successes.

Create a support group around you. Connect with a diverse range of people you can interact with and learn from. They will help you minimise mistakes and help you keep your sanity when the going gets tough. They will be the pillars you can lean on when your business seems to stop going the way you want it to.

What's Your Centre?

Often times it's when we are under pressure that our convictions are challenged and our standpoint grows stronger. It's as if we are tested by fire and the unimportant is burnt away leaving a pure, more refined version of who we are. It's in these times of challenge and growth that we can take our standpoint and craft a compelling vision. The more times we are tested, the purer the vision can become.

When each of my children were born, I experienced life lessons that have impacted my life from that point on. It's like I have been in a heightened state of contemplation about life and what's really important, and the rest just falls away. It was a fantastically overwhelming experience when Lisa gave birth to our first child, Max. It was a time to contemplate life, its responsibilities, and its meaning. After a long day visiting Lisa and baby Max, I was driving home from the hospital with my Mother-in-law, Pat. Lisa and I had not long been in our new home and Pat and I were chatting about it. We stopped at traffic lights in front of the local shopping centre and she said, "You're a bit further out than Mandy (my sister-in-law), aren't you?"

"No, we're actually a little closer to the city," I answered.

She responded, "I mean further from the Plaza."

At that moment it struck me. What was at my centre? What was the central point of my life? What was at the central point of my business? Clearly Pat thought living close to the shopping centre was important and I thought living near the city was important. For me, living near the shopping centre didn't even register on my list of priorities. Likewise, Pat has no desire to live near the city. Of course, neither of us centred our whole lives around these things, but it did get me thinking.

It's a cute little story I know, but it became particularly relevant a couple of years later when I confronted the most challenging time in my life. I will pick up the rest of this story later but, for now, I want you to consider the most important reasons for your business to exist. What is it at the centre of your life?

Eliminate Confusion

Most business people understand that having a vision is important. Vision gives you something to build a business towards. It guides all the decisions that you make throughout your business. The problem is, most people cannot easily communicate it, thereby making it ineffective.

Vision makes you consider the long-term strategy and not rely on ad-hoc impulses that can end up with you chasing the competition.

Without a clear vision, it's difficult to set goals that you can commit to long term. Be specific about what you want, so you know when you reach it. Instead of saying you want "more money" get specific about why you want more money. What are you going to do with it? How much more will it take?

If your vision is not simple, your business won't be either. Without clarity, you will be tempted to

"The ability to simplify means to eliminate the unnecessary so that the necessary may speak."

– Hans Hofmann

promise more than you can deliver, to change your message constantly, to redesign your website frequently, and modify your marketing strategy repeatedly. The confusion will exhaust you, your team will leave you, and you won't engage your target market effectively.

Clarity and simplicity are key components to SAs. This is particularly important online because website visitors don't take the time to absorb all your information. It needs to hit them straight between the eyes. Tactics and details may change as opportunities present themselves. However, your simple vision and unique standpoint should remain the same and become a rock solid foundation for your business.

Your vision will establish the basis for any future decisions. Ask yourself, "Will this decision enhance or hinder my vision?" You will find the decision-making process becomes simplified. It's like the decision was already made.

If your vision is simple, your team will pick it up quickly and feel more confident knowing your business is headed somewhere. Ideally they will feel a part of it and buy into the vision.

A common problem businesses face today is having stakeholders with different visions. Having more than one vision creates division. When there is no vision, decisions are made based on personal taste and opinion, rather than what is best for the business long-term.

Create a vision that works to your strengths and is congruent with your standpoint. You may have a certain skill, talent or knowledge that can be used to fulfil your vision. The more unique the better! You may have an unusual hobby or interest that could be the focus of how you do business. This would help you define a highly targeted niche. Your standpoint and vision must motivate and encourage you to pursue what you dream for.

If you don't know where you're headed in your business chances are that when you are faced with challenges you won't have the energy and resilience to keep moving forward. When you are tested by fire, chances are you will burn out.

What others perceive to be a distraction may potentially be your best focus. Distractions are fun, that's why we become absorbed by them. If you can create a business based on your favourite 'distraction', go for it!

While your business may be unique, if you want to achieve success you still need to understand the marketplace. Know who your main competitors are and what type of customers they target. Research can help you minimise risk, but more importantly, it helps you discover what makes you unique.

Discover what your competitors are doing and, if it doesn't make sense to you, do the opposite. We will cover this further in Lens 2.

Simplify Your Vision

Good quality products and services at a fair price are important – but that's an expectation. Every business should have this as a baseline. What makes you remarkable is your unique perspective or your vision.

SAs are constantly looking to maximise results and minimise workload. How do they do this? By making more promises, building new hopes, or introducing new KPIs (Key Performance Indicators)? No. By simplifying everything they do; and they start by creating a crystal clear vision. Individuals who become SAs usually do so because they love what they do and want to create their ideal lifestyle. A vision helps us imagine a better future and develop a strategy to reach our dreams. Your standpoint gives you perspective on what's important, it gives you a vision.

Old school businesses write up Mission and Vision Statements all the time. Most of these that I've seen are totally disconnected with the reality of the business they're meant to guide. They're filled with flowery language about how the business cares for the customers and believes in quality. They are so generic, they don't stir up any passion or conviction. They don't stand for anything unique, and therefore don't stand for anything at all! The missing ingredient is the unique standpoint upon which a vision should be built.

Defining a vision might sound a little cheesy to you. Call it something funkier if you need to, just make sure you do it. Your Vision Statement should be distinctive and strong so anyone associated with the business will understand and believe in it. You need to be able to articulate a unified set of values and core beliefs. Make it meaningful so it differentiates your business from that of potential competitors. Make it something you believe in and will be proud to put your name to.

Define why you do what you do. Know exactly what you believe and what you want to achieve. What's the end goal? What does it look like?

Creating your own defining vision can be a matter of simply "throwing it all at the wall" and seeing what sticks. It's all part of the brainstorming process. You don't need a complicated formula, you just need a pen and paper and to start dreaming.

To get started, ask yourself these questions:

- Why did I want to start my business?

- What kind of impact do I want to make on my customers?

- What kind of people do I want to work with?

- What's the most important thing I do in my business?

- What does the end result look like for my customers?

- What will customers value most in my business?

- What makes me unique in my industry?

- What is at the heart of what I do?

- What will I be compared to and how will I be different?

- What are the main benefits for my customers?

We are going to develop your business vision as you go through this book. Firstly, the questions above are not just part of an abstract exercise that businesses do without then using the insights in the daily running of the business. You will have generated a lot of ideas. Look for commonalities in your answers to the above questions. Is there something that keeps popping up? Brainstorm potential Vision Statements for your business and let the creativity flow. Refine your ideas into clear and direct messages. If one of these excites you and you can't get it out of your head you know you have a winner! Make it clear, simple, and audacious.

You will intuitively have a standpoint and vision for your business already, but it's helpful to clarify it so that it guides everything else within your business. With a clear vision everything becomes easier – marketing, decisions, everything. It will all become simpler, clearer, and more effective. Your target market will pick up on who you are and what you stand for. The more unique your standpoint, the easier it will be to communicate it with conviction. A business with a clear vision quickly becomes perceived as a major player in its niche. Why? Because you define or better yet, invent the niche.

Simplify your vision, or at least simplify the way you communicate it. As the business leader, you are the one to determine your vision. Choose something close to your heart that you are passionate about so it can sustain you in good times and bad. If you are already in business, a real eye-opener is asking your existing customers what they believe your business stands for. Ask them what they think is important to you as a business. Hopefully it's a close match to your own beliefs but they may articulate it in an unexpected way or emphasise aspects of your business which you may not have considered to be important. Let their thoughts inspire you, but don't let them dictate who you are and what you become. You decide.

Your vision must be something you maintain with passion and conviction, not some loose, generic rubbish you think your customers will want to hear.

"We don't see things as they are, we see them as we are."
– Anais Nin

If you find that your business has drifted away from the values you hold and the vision you believe in, devote some time to correct course. It doesn't need to be a complicated process, simply learn to communicate clear and concise messages that are always consistent with your unique standpoint.

Your vision should form the thoughts and feelings consumers get when they hear your business name. Some consultants tie all this in with branding. Branding this, branding that blah blah blah; they make it so complicated. Later in this book, I'll simplify branding for you and explore building a brand based on your vision.

Running a vision-driven business will save you time and money. Costs start to pile up when you focus on too broad a market, which is a result of not clearly defining your vision. As an entrepreneur, you must be specific in what you want to be known for. As an SA, you must stay focused and effective.

Your standpoint and vision should guide and shape all other principles in this book. It will govern your content marketing strategy, the design of your website, the way you use social media, and which organisations you get involved with. We will unpack these tactics for success later. For now, understand this: Decision making in all these areas becomes easier when you have a clearly defined standpoint. For example, your content marketing and social media strategies becomes easier because you have something unique and interesting to say that's worth sharing. It's not about posting what you had for breakfast. Nobody cares!

Make your online message interesting and informative, and address things that really matter such as:

- The major problems in your industry that you approach differently to your competitors

- Questions your customers have (or should have) that you can answer in a unique way

- The needs or desires your customers have that you can fulfil differently to competitors

A vision that is unique and aligned with your target market will be memorable and remarkable, making your ideas sharable. By being clear on what's important to you as a business, you can more easily create a lasting impression. If a prospect believes strongly in your standpoint, you will stay front of mind even if they are not ready to buy just yet. These are the customers that will become loyal advocates of your business. They are worth their weight in gold! Bring them in and include them in your vision. Let them feel a part of what you do.

People will be attracted to or turned off by your standpoint. Either way, that's okay. It saves you time and energy trying to qualify or disqualify people who may or may not become customers or join your team. You will get a "Yes" or "No" quicker, which saves time and is much better for everyone involved.

Your marketing message, both online and offline, becomes more focussed when you clearly define your vision. Don't be afraid to say the same message over and over again via different mediums. Few people will see or pay attention to all of them. Nobody is reading your material as much as you do, so you will become sick of it well before anyone else. People consume information in different ways. Some people love printed newsletters, some prefer email, some are addicted to social media. Experiment with different methods to see what your market engages with the most. Experimentation is a key to simplifying your business.

Unless you have a multi-million dollar budget, you need to play smarter than the larger corporations by being specific. SAs don't rely on huge budgets or people-power like large corporations do. They are able to grow organically by establishing a clear and unique direction for their businesses. You know it's crystal clear when everyone involved can articulate the vision, almost verbatim. Your vision should never hinder your flexibility and responsiveness to opportunities. There is no shortage of opportunities. Your vision should help guide what you pursue, and how you choose to pursue it. Because you know what you stand for, the direction to take becomes clearer and you can approach it in a responsive, dynamic way.

Your vision creates a perception of reliability. Reliable doesn't mean boring. Have fun in your business but make sure you have clarity in vision. When your vision is clear in your mind, it becomes clear to your target market and creates a sense of reliability and trustworthiness. It makes you the authority in the space you occupy within your industry. There's no point trying to communicate your reliability if you sacrifice your values for a quick buck. Your track record should always reinforce your vision with integrity. Reliability creates trust. Trust creates likeability. Likeability creates engagement. Engagement creates sales.

Wisdom of the Heart

What is the story of your business? Every vision has a backstory, and people connect with storytelling. If it is interesting, tell your prospects the reason for creating your business and what makes it unique. Everything in your business should support and enhances your vision: your logo design, your website, your brochures, the way you answer the phone. Everything! Vision comes with personality. Stand out from the crowd. Be impressive. Be remarkable. Your vision will become your unique selling proposition. Even if most of what you do is similar to what your competitors are doing, it's the one or two percent that you do differently that makes you unique and what matters most. What a powerful position to be in when you can say, "Yes, we do what our competitors do equally as well as them but let me explain what makes us unique."

People relate and understand concepts through story telling. Create a story for your business and its vision. Try to make it personal and interesting for people to relate to. What is the background to your business? Where have you come from and where are you going? What challenges did you overcome that support your message? How will your target market relate to it?

Your vision isn't all about you. It's about the people you will impact and the change you will make to your community. When engaging with your material your target market needs to clearly understand how your product or service benefits them, or benefits something of importance to them. Articulate your vision by emphasising the benefits it creates. Use benefits to set yourself apart. Benefits create emotional engagement with people genuinely interested in your offer. People buy the benefits.

> *There is a wisdom of the head, and a wisdom of the heart.*
> **– Charles Dickens**

There are three types of vision to consider. Understanding these three vision styles will help you formulate your own. Yours may be a combination of these, or it could be something completely different, if you are prepared to think creatively.

Ideological Vision

An ideological vision works on the highest level of consumer values. It's based on deep-seated beliefs that may have been held for a long time, even from childhood.

Success Vision

A success vision refers to personal or financial achievement gained from working with your business. This happens when a business creates a sense of success or victory. Some of the major global sporting companies focus on this simple principle.

Sociological Vision

A sociological vision comes from the satisfaction consumers feel from association with, or recognition of, your business. For example, driving a particular car or wearing particular clothing associates the consumer with a certain social group.

The key is to identify what style of vision is best suited to your business and what will be most compelling to your target market.

Reinventing Your Vision

It's the vision you believe in that defines your identity, not some branding strategy or clichéd Mission Statement. If you are already in business and think your current vision is not working well, maybe you haven't defined it clearly in your own mind or don't believe in it with your heart. You haven't tested it with fire. Of course, it could mean it's not perceived to be worthwhile by enough people to make a valid market. Sometimes a vision does require an overhaul. Be aware that consumers will find it hard to become familiar with your business if you change your vision frequently. Sticking with a single vision and then evolving its application over time is more effective than chopping and changing frequently.

Perception is everything. Whether you like it or not, what you say matters more than what you think, and what you do matters more than what you say. Although change can be daunting for some, SAs thrive on it because they are flexible, dynamic, and quick to capitalise on opportunity. While the underlying vision for your business will likely never change completely, the way you communicate it to the marketplace may. If there is a particular need or demand in the marketplace, you may emphasise different aspects of your vision in response to it. Not a complete change of direction, just a slight adjustment in light of the current environment or opportunities.

Reinventing your vision will keep your business fresh and innovative. Always be looking to be ahead of the trends. There will come a time when your business begins to look and feel dated. Maybe your logo looks like it was created in the 80's, or maybe your website doesn't have the functionality consumers have come to expect. Change is required and it's the perfect time to tinker with your vision. These minor changes give you an opportunity to adapt to the new, emerging marketplace.

Aim to maintain the core elements of your vision but give it a freshen-up. Show your customers you are remaining relevant. You don't need to do anything drastic to produce a significantly better result. What small steps can you take that will produce maximum results? You could go for a complete overhaul of your business but the truth is, in most instances, making some minor tweaks is a better use of your time and money. Complete overhauls are rarely in the best interest of a business looking to make changes. They are almost always in the best interest of the company recommending the changes, or the consultants and "experts" who thrive on major overhauls. When it's time for change, take care of it in bite sized pieces. If it feels

> *"If there are things you don't like in the world you grew up in, make your own life different."*
> **– Dave Thomas**

overwhelming to make the changes, procrastination sets in and you are likely to alienate your existing customer base in the process. Don't push away your existing customers; look for ways to transition them to the new aspects of your business seamlessly. If you're changing the course of your direction, consider how you can transition flawlessly so you don't distance your business from your customers in the process.

I'm going to do something dangerous in this book. I'm going to use case studies and examples of people I don't necessarily like or endorse. Learning from con-artists, cult leaders, and cruel political dictatorships isn't everybody's cup of tea. I'm not going to spend lots of time trying to qualify or disqualify their value systems; we will simply be looking for lessons we can learn from these extreme characters. Some readers may make the assumption that I believe in the same values these people do. What I value is learning from unlikely people in unconventional ways. It may even stir up passion within you and ignite your own convictions in opposition to some of the characters we explore. To make a difference in this world you've got to know what you support and you also need to know what you are against. You've got to be anti-something. What are you against? Let this passion drive you to bring change. Your standpoint may be defined by looking at the negative aspects of your industry and working out a way you can approach it differently to stand out from your competitors. If you can't stand something that is currently part of your industry and believe there is a better way, that's a great vision!

Here's a great example of how one guy's vision, determined by his childhood misfortunate, has become the catalyst for an amazing business. A friend recently introduce me to Jason Cunningham, author of "Where's My Money?" He is a genuine thought leader with regular gigs on TV and radio. I arranged to meet with Jason to pick his brain on what made him successful. We got chatting about his business and his history. He told me about a time when he was 11 and his father's business failed. His Mum and Dad lost everything and they all moved out of their nice house in Essendon into his Nan's home in the outer suburbs. The whole family lived in his father's childhood bedroom and in the evenings would assemble cheap jewellery and taps to make some money. Jason continued to go to a private school but was heckled by his peers when he was dropped off at school in a rundown old car. He was also heckled playing in his local footy team for being a private school pretty boy. It was a challenging time for Jason, but it became the catalyst for his success. Without doubt this experience shaped the direction of Jason's life. He wasn't going to let the lack of money dictate how his life would be. It wasn't always smooth sailing though. In his first year of business Jason and his business partner made $100 a month each.

At the time we met, they had a turnover of $8.5 million and he was confident that was going to grow. These days, Jason teaches a number of business principles to business owners, however he says that the two most important keys are having a clear purpose and values. These two keys seem to pop up whenever speaking with highly successful people no matter what industry they are in. I've heard religious leaders speak of similar principles, and no doubt political parties hold similar views. For Jason, purpose is about what you give, not what you get. He also defines it as a Mission Statement.

Values for Jason are about culture. It's about creating the right culture and purpose so everyone in the organisation 'gets it'. It's about creating a powerful 'Why'. Nobody cares about how you get stuff done, Jason says. All that matters is why you do what you do. Why is it important?

Standpoint Theory

I have been curious as to why people become so passionate about some standpoints, for example, Communism and Feminism. I am neither a Communist nor a Feminist, but I do find something compelling about people who have a unified, single-minded standpoint. When you dig a little deeper, and find out something about the culture these concepts are born out of, then you start to understand why they are passionate. They are often a response to some form of injustice. Those who uphold these standpoints have a valid, compelling reason why they adopted a certain way of thinking.

"Most people are other people. Their thoughts are someone else's opinions, their lives a mimicry, their passions a quotation."
– Oscar Wilde

Understanding comes when we are prepared to listen to people outside our usual networks, and people we don't necessarily agree with. At the time when these new concepts were released, they attracted their fair share of controversy. The system doesn't like to be challenged by new ideas because it threatens the status-quo. It's not a new concept to challenge conventional wisdom and stand up against the system. Jesus, over 2000 years ago, brought revolutionary ideas that challenged the thinking of the day. For us living in the western world, it can be difficult to grasp how controversial many of his statements were. He claimed to be God... I mean... that's a pretty big statement and one I happen to believe. He was considered a heretic by many for what he preached – enough to be brutally murdered – and he also had an agenda to 'set the capitives free'.

Maybe your small business won't revolutionise communities to the same extent as Communism, Feminism, or Christianity have; your business may not be fighting against oppression, inequality, or injustice to that level, but there are many lessons we can learn from this nonconformist approach. Which leads us to the next Lens...

nonconformist

Noun:

A person who does not conform to prevailing ideas or practices in their behaviour or views.

Synonyms:

dissenter, dissentient, protester, rebel, renegade, freethinker, apostate, heretic, schismatic, recusant, seceder, individualist, free spirit, maverick, unorthodox person, eccentric, original, deviant, misfit, hippy, dropout, fish out of water, outsider;

More: freak, oddball, odd fish, weirdo, bad boy, screwball, kook, wackadoo, wackadoodle

(Credit Google.com – Edited)

The School of the Con-Artist

If you want to create a unique business, don't learn from traditional sources. Learn from unexpected people and situations in unconventional ways. For example, there are many lessons we can learn from con-artists. They have an unconventional, nonconformist vision. They foresee potential problems and create solutions ahead of time to overcome obstacles. They are resilient, and think on their feet when the unexpected occurs. They do not allow themselves to be bogged down by the status-quo and are always looking for the next big idea. They want people to believe in them. That sounds a lot like SAs.

Don't get the wrong idea. I'm not proposing that you start conning customers, workers, or business partners. You can apply a con-artists unique abilities to your business without giving the law a reason to chase you down! For example, con-artists blend creativity, technology, and any other available tools to create effective results. Con-artists, like entrepreneurs, have the ability to think laterally and are forever looking for new tactics to improve their game plan and reach their end goal.

Start to think outside the proverbial box that has restricted far too many innovative minds over the years. Con-artists cannot be successful without thinking beyond the conventional. Their ability to have ideas that nobody else has considered before and use them to their advantage is exactly what SAs also do.

The modern business world is becoming increasingly challenging for 'me too' businesses – those that imitate other businesses around them and have nothing unique to set them apart. Don't become too comfortable with old ideas and systems. Consider how con-artists think up clever schemes that are only possible with out-of-the-box thinking.

Break the Rules. Conventional thinking and systems can be helpful to a point, but more often they hinder revolutionary ideas and breakthroughs. A certain disregard for rules, and being uncomfortable with restrictive conventions are the marks of visionaries. SAs aim to break rules not only to benefit their businesses but the customers they serve. Breaking the conventional methodologies can often provide game-changing results, without conning anybody.

Con-artists' are driven by their curiosity to explore. They explore the loopholes in systems, the psychology of their targets, and so on. If you wish to create a business that stands out from the crowd, use your curiosity to your advantage. Your curiosity can lead you to creating products and services that benefit your target market, not exploit them. Remember, if you are interested and inspired by a product or service, chances are someone else will be too.

Con-artists are known for their desire to take risks and accomplish seemingly impossible feats. They begin their work process by setting bold goals and creating strategies to achieve them, adapting as they make progress. They have a "never say die" attitude, and happily change the goals or methods as they go. There's a big lesson here for business owners since many fail in their first few years. If you want to succeed, have a "never say die" attitude. There will be challenges to overcome in business and you might need to refocus or aim the business at a different market. It's your job to find new, creative solutions.

You won't find any schools or universities that teach a con-artist how to become successful. But then again you won't find many entrepreneurs who have completed courses in Entrepreneurship either. Such courses do exist, however entrepreneurs often prefer non-conventional methods of learning. Con-artists and entrepreneurs have a constant craving for improving their craft. They learn what works, what doesn't, and are always on the lookout for opportunities to learn. Learning is an ongoing process for anyone who wishes to be successful.

On the flip-side, if you are ever done over by a con-artist you need to correct course and move on quickly. Becoming upset by a situation and letting it consume your thinking can be destructive for you emotionally, and for your business. Think back to Jack and the issues that consumed his thinking, leading him down a path of addiction and making him think his options were restricted. His thoughts and opinions are real for him and they are killing him. Don't let your mind be consumed by hate even when someone has done the wrong thing by you.

In my first-ever graphic and web design job, I saw the impact a con-artist can have – not so much by the money they steal but the hurt they cause people. We were a thriving, award-winning boutique marketing and design company in Sydney with a fantastic reputation. We were a small, dynamic team working on some great projects. I was loving it and it appeared most of the team were positive about their work situation too. Everything seemed to be going well until one day it was discovered the bookkeeper was conning the company out of money. From what I understand, she was running a crude little system of changing figures on paperwork and paying herself more every pay cycle. Once it was discovered she had done this once they tracked back and found she had been doing it for years.

As an outsider to all the nitty-gritty details of the situation, my perspective would probably be different to the business owners and management. However, it appeared to me that the discovery of this con-artist's theft began the downward spiral of the business. From this point the team slowly shrank until there were just two of us remaining. Very little new work was coming in – to the point that I had very little to do.

We moved into a small shared office in North Sydney and I was very unsure of the future of the business. It appeared to me that the con-artist became a distraction that zapped the energy of the leaders in the business. Up until the theft was discovered the business had been stolen from regularly, yet still managed to thrive.

It's my belief that it wasn't the theft that killed the business, it was the hurt and distraction that destroyed us. I don't know all the details but I know the issue was pursued in court. I doubt they ever got a penny out of the con-artist. Instead the whole situation cost them everything because they couldn't correct course and move on. If they had been thinking like entrepreneurs, or seeing the con as a learning tool, they could have refocused, and emerged from it stronger than ever.

What about the Haters?

Ignore the haters! Your business should be meaningful and relevant for your target market. Ignore the opinions of everyone else. Only you and your target market matters.

When you launch anything different to your competitors, you will attract knockers. Some people will listen and be persuaded by their arguments, but others will be curious to find out more about your business. Consider their comments free PR. It may help to understand your critics, but you don't need to be influenced by them. If they are existing customers with demands that will negatively affect how you run your business or how you work with others, cut them loose. The customer is not always right. As in any relationship, you may make mistakes and there may be times when you need to apologise and correct course.

> *"You have enemies? Good. That means you've stood up for something, sometime in your life."*
> **– Winston Churchill**

Managing and influencing your reputation, particularly online, can be a challenge for businesses who are genuinely unique. Forget about PR agencies, and forget about trying to appease the haters. There will always be haters that want to tear you down. For the most part you can ignore them. In fact, if you have a loyal following of customers online, they may run to your defence if they read something about you that they don't believe is true. That's a much better outcome than getting involved in the "argy-bargy". Create a fantastic customer experience and gently encourage them to share their experiences online. You want the positive experiences shared online to far outweigh any negative.

Some people won't like you and that's fine. If you know you are doing what you believe in, take the hatred as a compliment. It's an indication that you are on course!

The Internet, particularly social media, can be a great place for your business to flourish, but it's also a vulnerable place where your competitors can spy on you and attack you. Even people with no vested interest may get involved for no apparent reason. Trolls are everywhere. One blogger with a strong following can sometimes stir up trouble. They have a disproportionate amount of influence. It's best not to aggravate them!

You might be doing everything right, but some Muppet pops his head up with a negative comment. If someone searches for your business name online, what do they see? Hopefully all the first page listings are positive. I had a company contact me who were adamant they would never need a website and they held to this belief for years. Their particular industry and service didn't need a website as much as most businesses do. They were flourishing without one, turning over millions of dollars as a small business, until one catastrophic event changed everything. They were challenged by a legal matter that threatened to derail their reputation. Because they had no online presence at all, the court case details found its way to the top of all the major search engines when anyone typed their business name. Big problem. They thought nobody used the Internet to search for them, but they were wrong.

It became obvious it was causing problems after a few existing, loyal customers brought it up. After some thought, they did something they thought they would never do. They launched a website. They had one goal in mind, to push the negative publicity off the first page of the search engine results. We built a simple website and placed them on the major directories that were likely to push the negative pages down. Within a week, the problem was solved. That was a couple of years ago, and still today the negative information is pushed so far down the search results that it would rarely be seen by anyone. Complicated problem, simple solution. There was a whole lot more we could have done for them online but I don't believe in spending time convincing or persuading anyone to do more than they want to. They had a nonconformist attitude and I kind of liked it. Besides, there's far too much work out there to get bogged down with begging for it. Simply getting a website was a big step for these guys, and that was fine with me. I can't be sure if our client deserved the litigation or not, but I know we responded in a way that minimised the damage.

It can be helpful to directly respond to negative comments, particularly in social media, however you should never get caught up in a fight when someone attacks you. If you are being attacked on social media sites, blogs, or forums, it is best if you can take a diplomatic approach and thank them for the feedback. Don't get bogged down trying to vindicate yourself. Say sorry if it's appropriate, learn something if you need to, and move on quickly. Maintain a positive outlook built on the importance of your vision. Your vision should help you dominate your world. That doesn't necessarily mean you should destroy your competition. It's easier to dominate in your world by bringing others into it, rather than crushing them. It's about influencing and redefining the market according to the rules you create.

Personality and Perceptions

Boring businesses don't get noticed by anyone. It's better to have some people that love you, and others that hate you, than to be ignored. Bland businesses do not bring change. Bland businesses do not grow. Staff don't want to work there, customers don't want to shop there.

When you stand for something, it defines who you are on the inside. Who you are on the inside is presented through your personality. Even shy or insecure people seemingly grow in personality when they speak about something they are passionate about. The importance of the message becomes the driving force that helps them break out of insecurities.

"Logic will never change emotion or perception."
– Edward de Bono

Distil your vision down to a minimal amount of words that can be easily understood and remembered. It could be a single statement, or it could be few bullet points. There's no set formula. There's only one rule – that you own it.

Build rapport with your target market on a personal level. Let them see what your business exists for. Be seen as a credible and honest business they can trust. Welcome feedback from everyone, not so you can be pushed around and be told what to do by the vocal minority, but so you become aware of any blind-spots and understand opposing views to your own. If you are a nonconformist there should be plenty.

Many business owners are nervous about being too 'out there'. They also worry about targeting a specific niche because they don't want to miss out on other opportunities. It's a scarcity mindset. Don't let it bind you. The danger of this kind of thinking is that you'll make your business too generic and become just like all your competitors. By being specific you know exactly who you are and who you want to work with. It makes it easier to attract these kinds of people. By focusing on a specific target market, you become unique and can present a consistent personality. Your personality will get you noticed, and that creates momentum others are swept up by. You'll get some customers completely at random for no apparent rhyme or reason. That's cool too, as long as they don't dilute what you are doing for your ideal customers.

Perceptions and Your Authentic Self

Perception is reality. We may not like it but it's true in many aspects of business. The way you present your business goes a long way in forming the perceptions you create.

The perceptions of your business are directly related to the amount of respect your business can create. Remember the con-artist we were learning from? They only focus on what people perceive. Making something unique and special about your business means you don't have to compete on price alone. The uniqueness can come from the product or service itself, however that can be restrictive. If your product is genuinely unique and profitable, it won't be long before someone comes along to copy it and undercut you. You can try to protect your

Intellectual Property (IP) but it often costs a fortune to defend. If the big boys want to copy you, they have deep enough pockets to do so. You can't rely on the uniqueness of your product or service alone. The only thing they can't easily copy is You. Your unique personality. Your authentic self. Those little quirks nonconformists tend to have are very difficult to replicate. While competitors may try and copy your vision, they will skip over the underlying DNA you have as the originator and find it's not so easy to replicate your passion. It can never be just about products and services.

> *"You can mass-produce hardware; you cannot mass-produce software - you cannot mass-produce the human mind."*
> **– Michio Kaku**

Don't think of products or services as a set of items but solutions to problems. Tangible and intangible elements of your business come together to create an experience. Customers build a relationship with your business through the experiences you create. Be true to yourself as a business and as an individual. Be your authentic self. It seems like all the small businesses try to appear big while the big businesses try to appear small and more personal. If you are a small business, use it to your advantage.

Why not build the business around your own identity and personality? Use your name and photo where appropriate. Since many of the relationships are probably built with you personally, why not leverage that advantage? Some people I have suggested this to say they don't want to remain a small business, therefore they don't want the business to be built around them or their personality. I understand that, however we can build upon what we already have going for us. Even some large organisations build their businesses around the owner's identity – think Richard Branson. He hasn't done too badly using this method for growth.

It helps to humanise your business by defining its personality. Determine its gender, age and social class. What does it like and dislike? What does it do for fun? This may sound a little unorthodox, however it will help you visualise your business personality so you can better define it.

How do my customers presently see my business?

You will have a feel for this based on your day-to-day dealings with customers. Large corporations don't have this advantage since the decision makers are so far removed from the coalface where the customer interaction occurs. If you are not sure how they see your business, prompt your customers to provide testimonials. They will naturally highlight what they see as important in your business.

Get testimonials to publish, and you get great customer research done for you in one go. Some may refuse to provide a testimonial, that's normal. If most of the people you approach refuse, that could be a sign they haven't bought into your vision and it needs work.

How do you want your customers to see your business?

Think of your business and its personality like you would a human relationship. Think about your business personality and how your customers will engage with that style of personality. Always be yourself but consider who you are engaging with. You already adjust the way you present yourself when speaking to different people according to who they are and the relationship you have. In the same way, adjust how you present your personality according to who you are engaging with as a business. Your relationships need to be nurtured while they grow.

Continually look at your business from a fresh, nonconformist perspective. If your business was a person, how would it answer these questions?

- What kind of clothing would you wear?

- What would you do for fun?

- Where would I find you?

- What would your favourite colours be?

- What kind of music would you listen to?

- Who would you want to work with?

- Who would you follow on social media?

- Who would you hang out with?

There are many other questions you could ask in this way. Be playful. Let your mind wander and see where it leads. Your business personality will often lead to mental pictures. Don't ignore this imagery. Create illustrations and draw diagrams.

Many of us are visual learners and will understand concepts more easily when images are used. Even if you are not artistic, draw what you see, jot it down, get the crayons out, whatever it takes to remember your ideas. They may also be helpful when having visual material developed, or when briefing a graphic designer if you need a logo designed. Also, they are good to revisit from time to time to see if your business became your original vision.

Who you are as the leader of your business goes a long way in forming what your business becomes. Your business must be congruent with your own personal beliefs and values, not just something you think will make you money. Focussing on money alone will not sustain you long-term and the marketplace will see straight through your lack of authenticity. Remember that it's not about being a slick sales peddler, it's about relationships.

Under-promise and over-deliver. It's a cliché but it's rarely achieved. When you go above and beyond the minimum service level, your business is the winner. It's about perceived value. It isn't always evident to customers that they have received additional value, so discretely bring attention to any additional value you have provided. Balance your aspirations with the reality of what you can currently offer as a business. Make it believable. Make it authentic. Authenticity is what creates long-term success because it creates trust, generates positive word-of-mouth, and brings in repeat business.

- What kind of personality will best suit your business?

- Are you a BMW or a Ford?

- Are you a McDonalds or a fine-dining restaurant?

- Do you want your business to be seen as a 'rock star' or a 'dependable friend'?

- What are you competitors doing and can you be the opposite?

Sacking Your Customers

Keeping customer satisfaction high does not mean you should keep every customer. Some customers simply are not suited to your business and will waste your time and energy that could have been better spent with others who are more suitable. If they are not suitable, find a way to move them on to somewhere thats a better fit for them. I do this from time to time to keep our service levels high and prices competitive for our good customers. When a customer is discovered to be not suited to your business, be careful how you treat the transition. Refer them to a competitor who may be a better fit or try to help them transition in some other way. It's in everyone's best interest to keep it amicable. A discontented customer can do a lot of damage to your business through negative word-of-mouth even when you don't deserve it. Be prepared to take a small loss on the poor quality customer. Keep them happy in the transition. If they feel they are the winner out of the experience, it's a worthwhile investment despite the cost to you.

What you say 'No' to is as important as what you say 'Yes' to. By trying to supply a product or service that isn't the best option for the customer, you may create negative commentary and won't enjoy your work. Stick with what you are good at, and do it well. Your intention should be to provide a solution worth raving about. Be selective with who you work with and communicate that clearly with the marketplace so they can self-assess if they should be working with you or not. It will save you time and money dealing with people who were never a good fit for you in the first place. When you're specific in what you want, you'll be able to identify a bad fit more easily and be able to send them elsewhere, before they cause you heartache and waste your time.

> *"We are not trying to entertain the critics. I'll take my chances with the public."*
> **– Walt Disney**

For example, my business, Omnific Design, choose not to work with every business that contacts us. We partner closely with our clients and therefore published these three rules on our website:

1. We need to be confident your business model can be successful online. Our reputation of producing websites that create profit is at stake, and we can't allow that to be affected by a poor quality business idea.

2. If we believe a business does not provide a good product or service we will not work with them. The online strategies we implement are proven to produce leads and sales, so we feel morally obligated not to mislead consumers into buying a poor product or service.

3. If we find some other ethical reason why we don't want to partner with a company, or simply don't feel it's a good fit for us, we will let the company know. We are in a privileged position where we can be a little selective with what clients we take on-board.

Bigger Isn't Always Better

A bigger business is better than a smaller one, right? They'll get the work done faster and do a better job since they have more resources than a smaller business. Oh really?

Far too often, small businesses try to act bigger than they are, while the bigger companies try to appear smaller. As a small business it's good to dream big and look to grow, however this doesn't necessarily mean increasing staff numbers, and it certainly shouldn't mean sacrificing the advantages you have by being small. Small businesses have the ability to respond to opportunity quicker and more effectively than larger businesses who are bogged down with systems and paperwork. While they're holding meetings trying to get something new off the ground, you can take advantage of the situation and get started light and lean, and create momentum.

Your impulses can be good. While large corporations need to qualify and justify everything, when launching something new they still base their judgements on assumptions. Guess what? Their assumptions can be as wrong as someone acting seemingly on impulse alone, using intuition. Large corporate 'decision makers' will bring in consultants for just about everything, so they don't have their head on the chopping block if it goes bad. It's the old, "It wasn't me, they told us to do it!" mentality.

What a horrible existence these corporates have. I'd rather drive rusty nails into my eyeballs. As you can imagine, the consultants start by outlining what everyone else is doing, and soon the company is following everyone else. Entrepreneurs know that impulsive decisions often come from intuitive insight based on years of experiences. You may not be able to qualify or articulate those insights well, but that doesn't make them any less powerful, or less right. Don't let the hoop-jumping antics of the large corporates persuade you to run your business their way. I'm not suggesting you throw all your time and effort into an impulsive idea. Firstly, ask yourself how well the idea fits with your vision. If it's a good fit, sit on it for a day or two and start off small so you can experiment with those ideas. It's about testing your assumptions in the real world, not based on some consultant's generic ideas. You'll make educated guesses like the big companies do, but you'll do it faster and more cost-effectively. As a small business, you have your finger on the pulse more than bulky corporations do – you know what customers need. This enables you to discern more about the market you're involved in.

Big businesses are often slow and clunky with mountains of paperwork and procedures. To get even the simplest task done can be a challenge. The economies of scale can tip in your favour as you grow, but it does come at a cost. Small lets you keep your systems lean so you can adapt as opportunities present themselves.

Loyalty and Broken Promises

"I began revolution with 82 men. If I had to do it again, I do it with 10 or 15 and absolute faith. It does not matter how small you are if you have faith and plan of action."

– Fidel Castro

When presented to the market, your business will create expectations. Strong businesses create strong promises, both directly and assumed. Be sure you can deliver on the promises you're making. What you deliver must match or exceed customer expectations. Provide abundant value to your customers.

Do you always deliver on your promises?

From time to time, all of us fail to deliver what we promised, when we promised it. Despite our best intentions, things happen outside our control. Maybe you promised to deliver something by email before noon but the Internet bombed out. Maybe the product you shipped was damaged in transit.

When problems hit, apologise to your customer and more importantly, work out how you can resolve the issue now; and how you can work around the challenges better next time. There isn't always a solution, however it's about maintaining the integrity of your business. Whenever possible, learn to foresee problems and solve them before they become an issue.

As an entrepreneur, you probably have a high tolerance to change. However, many people crave consistency. That's what keeps most of the population working a regular day job. Take their need for consistency into consideration and keep them informed, especially when there are delays or unforeseen problems that arise. The most important things are perceptions and relationships, so be honest and upfront.

Your customers want to be able to rely on getting the same high-quality experience from your business every time. It's crazy how much some people crave consistency. They will prefer to go to a drive-thru takeaway outlet than try something they haven't eaten before because they enjoy knowing what to expect. They know it's probably not the best option, but they don't want to 'risk' being surprised or disappointed. If people are resistant to taking risks in such small decisions, they may have a melt-down when faced with more important issues. It's not your job to change your customers' personality and preferences. Create a consistent experience for them so they know what to expect, each and every time.

You know you have a great vision when you have a tribe of loyal customers who believe in you and your business. The ultimate test of your vision is the loyalty it creates. If you have a strong vision that is hitting the mark, even when something goes pear-shaped, your loyal customer will stick with you because they believe in what you stand for. Relationships built on shared beliefs create bonds that are not as easily broken as an emotionless business transaction. Even if your prices are slightly higher than your competitors, customers will stick with you because they believe in what you do. The bond linking your customers and your business is foundational to the strength of your business.

From time to time you will be challenged as a business. There will be new competition, and new products and services that compete for your target market. In tough times you will learn the true value of your uniqueness. To help you determine the strength of your business ask yourself:

- What are the problems I solve for customers?

- What are the solutions I provide for my customers?

- What are the benefits of my product or service for my customers?

- What emotions do my customers feel using my product or service?

- What makes my business meaningful and something people want to be involved with?

What I Learnt Growing up in a Cult

Our experiences as children largely shape the way we view the world. Growing up in a cult certainly had an impact on me. It was a religious group that I would describe as legalistic. They had a growing list of rules for just about everything you would ever do in life. It wasn't particularly dangerous – harmless mostly. No doubt the leaders had good intentions for the followers by helping them avoid what they believed were poor decisions, but that meant it was controlling. There were many common systems that you will find throughout many cults. Systems make cults successful. These are systems your business can learn from... of course, I hope you use this knowledge for good not evil!

Cults use manipulative techniques to convince and persuade people to their way of thinking. While I don't endorse manipulation, which has negative connotations, I do endorse influence. The success of SAs is often built on the influence they create. They influence their team members, and they influence their target market. They continually build their influence. Influence is the currency of SAs.

I know cults vary from group to group, however the one I grew up in was not about tricking anyone or using mind control. They genuinely believed in what they preached. SAs must also genuinely believe in what they preach. It all comes back to your standpoint, vision, and creating influence around your belief system.

Destructive cults sell the benefits of joining the group to the new believer and once their commitment is established, shift the focus to what's better for the leader and the beliefs of the group. It's extraordinary what can be done once control is established over a group of devotees, even to the point of mass suicide as occurred in the Heaven's Gates group, a bizarre UFO religion from California. It's not likely the Heaven's Gates cult would have had many followers if they were told upfront "wear these weird clothes, get castrated and drink this poison: it's going to be great!"

As SAs, we must be fully transparent and remain focused on the benefits for our customers. Unlike cults, we don't live in an isolated environment which we control. We live in a world open to free thinking, and that's how it should be. Manipulation will not work long term, outside of a tightly controlled environment.

The cults I've studied place a high value on recruiting others to believe in the system. They use a variety of recruitment techniques that have been developed over time. They learn what appeals most to their target audience at the various stages of them becoming involved. Like the con-artist, they focus on allowing people to believe in them.

SAs use similar techniques to encourage others to spread the news about their products or services. They move their market through deeper levels of commitment. For example, customers buy the $30 product, then the $300 more in-depth product, and finally the full immersion program that might require investing a few thousand dollars.

Cults don't always live in communes and wear strange clothes, in fact most don't. They look like everyday people. Most of us think we are immune to becoming involved in a cult or being manipulated by others, but it happens all the time.

It happens in the business world too. An unsuspecting person will attend a free event knowing the presenter will be selling something on the day. A training program, a DVD set, a new system, a better life, or a better future. The unsuspecting person will resolve that they won't buy anything, and that they will learn from the free session and move on.

The free event is jam packed with useful, inspiring content. The person presenting is engaging and believable. The room is buzzing with excited, happy people who love the leader. Better yet, the offer is value-packed and it comes with the promise of a better future.

Before long the cult leader... I mean business speaker... has won the hearts and minds of the attendees. They close with their offer and have people running to the back of the room for a special deal.

The unsuspecting person is swept away in the excitement and promise of a better future and follows the crowd to the back of the room, credit card in hand. As it turns out, they were not immune to the influence of the cult/business.

Cults around the world have millions of followers. Some have bizarre beliefs, yet highly educated people are convinced to believe in them. Doctors, lawyers, CEO's, movie stars... nobody is immune.

Cults are built around a belief system, as are successful businesses. For you it can be The Simple Manifesto and the ideas that are born out of it. For other businesses, it could be a whole range of ideologies. Problems arise when you are not rock solid in your belief system as a business.

Cults will often create powerfully emotional experiences. Good salespeople also understand customers buy emotionally. They will encourage you to think about how your life will be better with their product or service. They might say "What would it mean to you if our products provided you an additional $20,000?" "How would you use that additional income?" "What would that mean to your family?" "How would that make you feel?" It could be about more money, more time, a better lifestyle, anything that people crave. If you can make them picture it and dream about it, you can create an emotional response.

Even political parties have used cult-like methods. Consider the Nazi party in years gone by. The passion and dedication they could stir up around a set of beliefs is frightening. Terrorists, racial supremacists, and other rebel groups are able to build a movement around a set of ideals. Opposing views often enhance the resolve of the group. Feeling like the minority tends to make these groups even more passionate to push their agenda. Create for yourself a set of ideals that set you apart in your industry. Competitors may consider these ideals crazy, yet the differences can work in your favour.

Cults use the fear of loss as a motivating tool to keep members on-board. If you don't give us money, you will be cursed. If you quit, you will lose your friends and family. If you quit, you will go to hell. To a degree this was how it worked in the group I grew up in. When you leave, members are told not to "fellowship" with you because you are the backslider. They tell them you have been handed over to the Devil for your sin. This traps other people into staying.

Business can use the fear of loss too, hopefully not in such a manipulative way. If a customer or client moves on to use a competitor's product or service, they won't get the "secret sauce" only you can provide. Your competitive advantage should be strong enough that customers are aware of what they miss out on if they leave. They may save a bit of money by going to your competitors, but they lose the relationship they have built up with you and the extra something that only you can provide.

Cults create a sense of superiority. You can only be "saved" within their system. The mainstream "compromise" the enlightening beliefs that the cult holds onto. This was common when I was growing up in the cult. Leaders would openly ridicule other groups and mock their beliefs. The difference between them and us, was what made us feel superior.

Think about your difference when marketing your business. Chances are your prospects have already bought into the idea that they need a product or service similar to yours. Your competitors probably sold them that idea. You only need to sell the part that makes you unique. This is what makes you superior. They will either buy into it or not. Either way the decision-making cycle is faster and you will be competing less on price and more on perceived value. If your customers believe in your superior option, it creates loyalty. No longer are they shopping for a cheaper price because they understand they cannot get what you offer elsewhere.

Cult leaders build an inner circle of "Yes Men" around them. A group of people seen to be elite. The exclusivity becomes something others aspire to. Your business can also create an inner circle, a group of customers or clients who buy into a premium version of what you offer. These people are often early adopters and become loyal followers and raving fans who draw others into your business.

Cult leaders create authority within their community because they create the environment and the rules at play. When SAs create their own community, they also create the environment and rules.

Cult leaders have unhealthy control over their members. I remember sitting through many "talks" which outlined what we could and could not do. I remember hearing the leader in Melbourne say playing sports was not encouraged because it takes people away from the fellowship. At Christmas and Easter, we would go to camps with the other members. There were meetings throughout the day where they told us about more and more activities that were not acceptable.

Questioning the leadership in any way was seen to be rebellious and you would be disciplined for creating discourse in the assembly. The public embarrassment of excommunicating members for a few weeks for some kind of sin was common. The gossip amongst members must have been torturous for the poor victims. Guilt, character assassination and shame were the motivators.

On another occasion there was a meeting for youth and the leaders asked everyone to close their eyes while they called out various sins. The attending youth needed to confess by raising their hands. They told us they would know anyway so it's best we confessed there and then. It was at that meeting, I realised how weird it all was and that I would not be a part of it any longer.

Manipulation through fear is often used as a tag team with "love bombing" tactics. Cults understand the power of relationships. If they can control your relationships, they can control you. When you first get involved with a cult you may find you get instant friends. How could such wonderful people be bad? These so-called friends are intent on indoctrinating you. Over time, they begin to discourage your other relationships with friends or family. You will become more and more dependent on your new friends and eventually become trapped by the fear of losing them. Cults want to minimise external influences and friends and family are, of course, a significant influence in most people's lives.

Multilevel marketing (MLM) groups are often considered commercial cults. They rely on greed to recruit people and use a range of deceptive tactics. Those that join are typically instructed to sell to their friends and family. It's a fast way to burn relationships, and most people make little money in these schemes. They will probably try to get you to come to lengthy information sessions, and some will avoid telling you the company name until the end. You have got to wonder about organisations that won't openly tell you their name. I do not encourage you to join any MLM group, but you may want to attend their recruitment meeting to learn some of the strategies that make their recruitment processes successful. Be prepared to get your defences up to avoid being sucked in.

Let's Get Emotional

Get inside your customers' heads. People spend their money based on their emotions and the perceived benefits of the product or service. It is worth considering the following:

- What do the people who need your product or service value?

- How does your product or service make them feel?

- How do they feel if they don't have your product or service?

Emotions are the strongest motivator for any customer. Engage your prospects on an emotional level. Understanding the benefits, and the emotions associated with those benefits, enables you to become relevant to your prospects and gain their interest. Consider what features will matter most to them, not to you. Features drive decisions only when the benefits are clearly understood.

What features and benefits will catch your prospects' attention quickly?

As we learnt from the cult leaders, people tend to buy for emotional reasons, and then rationalise their decision to justify their purchase. Here are some common emotional drivers that can be used to engage your target market:

Excitement

Excitement has a big impact on your market's buying decision and creates a strong desire for your product or service.

Security

Security is a strong emotional reason for a consumer to buy a product or service. Using a warranty, guarantee, or promise will help stir this emotion.

Fear

Consumers don't want to feel like they might lose a good deal. A sense of urgency can create the fear of missing out. The fear of what could potentially happen if a consumer doesn't make a purchase is also a significant driving force. Insurance is an excellent example as it's almost always purchased due to fear of the unknown.

Convenience

Consumers are willing to pay for convenience. If your product or service is more accessible than your competitors', highlight that fact.

The Simple Manifesto

Pleasure, Pain, and Purpose

Let's be honest, most people are seeking pleasure and trying to avoid pain, but they are also searching for meaning and purpose. Give them pleasure, remove pain, and offer them purpose through your messages. Present them with the promise of a better future.

What's in a Name?

If you haven't yet launched your business, then ideally you'll create a name that highlights what makes you unique. For example, if your point of difference was based on getting your product to customers faster than competitors, it's a good idea to name it something that showcases your speed. Pull out the thesaurus, or log onto an online version, and see what words you can come up with that will represent your vision well. If you're already in business, and already trading under a business name, then it's often best to stick with what you have, and create a tagline to emphasise your point of difference.

When choosing a name for your business, there are no right or wrong answers. It's usually best to keep it short, simple, and easy to spell. If it's memorable and playful, it will offer opportunities for fun marketing and advertising ideas. You could also merge a couple of words to create your business name. For example, look at Microsoft. The words Micro and Software are both common in the computer world. Another example is Facebook. It began as a place where people could post a photograph of their face and read each other's profiles and comments, like a book.

It's great if your business name lends itself to mental pictures that help people remember it. Acronyms don't usually work because they are often cold and meaningless to the consumer. They can work however if the acronym is also an acrostic (word puzzle, or other composition in which certain letters in each line form a word or words) that is a great name in its own right.

Be sure to check the availability of the website domain name. If the domain is not available you could find out who is holding it and see if you can buy it, but it could be an expensive process. If you can't get the domain name to match your business name, then you should consider another name. You may also want to check social media availability for your name. For tools to help you do this, visit www.simplemanifesto.com/members (The Access Code is SNAP)

> *"No one is any one thing."*
> **– Martin Short**

Of course you'll need to make sure you can legally use and register the name, so get some legal advice. This book is not the place for legal advice.

Question Authority

Always question people who are believed to be authorities. This is not necessarily something you need to do publicly – you don't always need to confront anyone. The SA knows that it's important to challenge preconceived ideas and assumptions. Beliefs and understandings in all spheres of life are passed down from person to person, and generation to generation but they are not always valid. As we all know, they can be very wrong.

Because it's been a certain way, doesn't mean that's the only way. It may not even be the best way. Most of the time you will be able to question assumptions internally, and make your own decisions on how to run your business and life. Sometimes you will need to raise the issue with the people involved if it impacts your life or business in any way. Sometimes you will need to take a risk, and do what you know is right. That's why you are an SA.

When challenging conventional wisdom it's not just to prove them wrong, but to give them the opportunity to prove themselves right. Remain open minded, they may have some valid thoughts and reasons why it is the way it is. Then again, they may not. Even if they do have compelling reasons, there may be equally compelling reasons to try a different approach. Some will label you rebellious and stubborn. If you have valid ideas that are different to theirs, and they are not prepared to listen or be open, then who is the stubborn one? Who cares anyway? If you're going to do anything remarkable, you will polarise people. Some will love you for your convictions, others will hate you. That's better than being a cookie-cutter, run-of-the-mill, struggling, small business owner.

When you fight for what you believe in, you own it. It becomes part of the fabric of who you are. It also makes a great story, which is great bait for the media. I've seen it time and time again. Someone stands up and challenges the way it's been in the past. They share their ideas with passion and conviction and quickly build a following of people who buy into the new, exciting ideas. These people who buy-in often start to share the same set of ideas, using the same phrases, language, analogies, and even presentation style of their thought leader. In some circles of influence, I've even seen accents change slightly to replicate the leader from another country such is the respect they have for their leader. It becomes a movement when the second generation of leaders join in and grows quickly.

The momentum is not always sustainable, often relying on the original thought leader. The second generation leaders may spruik the same messages, almost verbatim, but they didn't fight for them, therefore they don't own them with the same conviction. When a leader owns what he or she shares, even if their presentation style isn't as polished, their believability is high and others want to get involved.

There is something unique and special about someone who has fought for his or her convictions. That part of them cannot be easily replicated or taught. It needs to be fought for. There may be those who try to copy your business model, but they cannot copy your identity. This is why you should fight for what you believe in, it's compelling.

In business, if you're challenging your industry with a new standpoint, a new product or service, then you probably need to fight for it. People may not quickly understand why your business is a better alternative to what they have experienced previously. Learn to articulate the reasons why in a compelling way. Know that the fight will make you the leader in your niche. You own the space.

When handing on your business to a successor, they have two options. Firstly, they can rely on the momentum you created to sustain them. It may be a solid, consistent business, and that's fine. The other option is to rechallenge the marketplace, building upon what you established. Chances are, if what you have created is a great business, there will be copycats, so rechallenging the market may be the best way forward. By the third generation, you'll almost certainly need to reinvent the business unless you're happy with mediocrity. Questions to consider include:

> *"You can either be informed and your own rulers, or you can be ignorant and have someone else, who is not ignorant, rule over you."*
> **– Julian Assange**

- What generation is my business in right now?

- Is it time to challenge the industry?

- Is it time to reinvent my business?

Mind-Numbing Market Research

Many small businesses become overwhelmed trying to understand their market. They often get stuck on demographics such as income, location, gender, age, relationships, hobbies, and interests. Gathering a whole lot of data around these attributes may be of some value, but it doesn't need to be so complicated. For the small business owner or entrepreneur who has a hands-on working relationship with customers, it could be as simple as reviewing your best few clients and working out what similar attributes they share. That way you can create marketing to attract more people like them.

Large corporations allocate huge amounts of money for market research. They need to, because the decision makers don't have hands-on, face-to-face experience with actual customers who they can listen to and learn from. Big business understands the importance of understanding the market in order to successfully communicate with prospects and customers. For most small businesses, this level of research would send them broke before they even get started. This is not to say the same principles can't be achieved on a smaller scale.

If you are just getting started and think you know exactly what your prospects' need or want, you could be wrong. Get started and find a fast, cheap, and effective way to test assumptions as you progress. As customers come on board, ask them for feedback.

If you are new to business and don't have a customer base to draw ideas from, brainstorm with other entrepreneurs and creative thinkers. External perspectives are always valuable since we can often get too close to our own projects and lose sight of the bigger picture.

You could conduct sophisticated research and surveys, however if you are a small business with direct customer contact, you shouldn't need to. Conversational feedback is always best, and you'll pick up common trends quickly. Be mindful not to be persuaded by the vocal minority. It may be only a minority complaining about an aspect of your business while the majority love what you do but don't say so.

Spy on your competitors. Look at the most successful businesses in your industry. What makes them so successful? Try to get your hands on as many brochures and other sample material as you can. Websites are easily accessible and often give you insight into your competitors' strategies. This will allow you to pick up their marketing messages, and identify what works for them, not so you can copy what they do. Actually, it may be the opposite. You may discover opportunities your competitors have missed.

Make Your Competition Irrelevant

Become a specialist in your industry. Specialists earn more than General Practitioners because it's assumed they are the best at what they do. If you are a nonconformist, you should be the only one doing what you do. It's called niche marketing. By focussing on a niche, you become the go-to person for your specific product or service. Niche marketing is simply focusing your business on one segment of the market. By focusing on a niche, you can distinguish specific needs and benefits your target market is interested in. We are inundated with marketing message like never before. Niche marketing helps SAs cut through the noise. It's about being a big fish in a small pond.

Stop trying to sell your product or service to everyone and start selling to someone specific; someone who is interested and will listen. Focus on a particular kind of person. This allows the message to be created specifically to engage that type of person.

Don't try to compete in the marketplace the same way multi-national companies with multi-million dollar marketing budgets do. Get involved in one specific niche and maximise it. The more specific you are, the less complicated your business will be, and the less competition you will have. Competitors who focus on a broad range of products or services will become irrelevant because you are considered the specialist, and the only logical choice for what you do.

Mainstream businesses and large corporations often overlook small but profitable niches. They may not be interested in smaller niche areas because their overweight business models require a larger number of customers to make it sustainable. They are big, fat, slow, and complicated. As an SA, keep your business model lean, agile, and simplified so you can exploit these often-overlooked opportunities.

There are many elaborate marketing methods, strategies, and systems available these days, however niche marketing creates clarity and an easily defined purpose. Sounds simple I know, but it's interesting how many businesses don't deliver a clear message. Your simple message should highlight:

- The benefits of using your product and service

- What your prospects should do next (i.e. call-to-action).

You need a clear, compelling message to prompt your prospects to make a decision and act immediately. Many business owners try to squeeze as much information as they can about every single product or service they provide into a marketing piece, and then wonder why nobody responds. When trying to say 'everything' about your business, your message becomes complicated and confusing. By trying to communicate too much, you communicate nothing at all.

Many business owners believe they have a clear direction for their marketing however, when you ask them to articulate their marketing message, they struggle to give a clear, concise response. Try to provide simple answers to the following questions:

- What makes people buy your product or service?

- Why should you be trusted?

- What makes you the better choice over the competition?

These questions are a great place to start when creating a marketing message for your niche. Your message must answer the needs and desires of your niche. When you create a clear, powerful marketing message, you can adapt it for a variety of purposes. Every piece you produce is an opportunity to reinforce your message.

Selecting your niche doesn't need to be a complicated, time-consuming process. It often paralyses small businesses who then never take action. Get started, and test the waters with clients to see what you enjoy and are most successful doing. As your business and experience grows, your niche will develop, and your marketing will evolve. Don't fight the change; embrace it, enhance it, and continue to make incremental improvements. The next chapter will help you understand what makes your niche market tick, so stay tuned...

Often the most productive niche is the one that you evolved into over time. If you are already in business, start with the people already on your customer list and let the niche develop from there.

Often your niche will be based around your own personal interests.

> *"You don't get any points in life for doing things the hard way."*
> **– Tim Fargo**

- What are you most passionate about?

- What personal interest do you have that could become your niche?

A niche market opportunity exists where there is a common motivation felt by your prospects which causes them to be interested in your products or services.

If you are currently serving a broad range of customers, which niche is the most profitable?

Start out with one specific niche and as you reach capacity, look to leverage it to approach related market niches. Reworking a product, service, or marketing system, to serve a new niche is a much easier task than starting from scratch. There may be tinkering required, but the bulk of the work will already be done. Rinse and repeat. It's that simple!

Unconventional Customer Profile

Please don't assume the shortness of this chapter means it's less important than other chapters. The fact is, it's short because it's simple to implement yet powerful if you try it. I encourage you to find a way to apply the ideas, here and build a successful business from the results.

There are many complicated systems and processes out there to help you create an ideal customer profile. They endorse ample research and analysis, which of course, requires the services of the consultant endorsing the system. What if I told you there is an easier way, that is no cost and can be a lot of fun? Would you believe me? It can be. This process identifies the psychology behind your ideal clients. The basic demographics can be easily identified too.

Don't get bogged down with complicated details, simple points like location, age, and gender should all be easy to work out. Company size in terms of turnover or staff numbers have some value, but nothing compares to the psychology behind the decision makers. It's the simple human element that matters most.

Here are 8 simple steps:

1. If you are in business already, hand pick the best half dozen or so customers you have now. These are the people you love working with, and/or are the most profitable. If you haven't yet begun, either select a few people you know who are the type of people you would like to work with, or imagine the type of person you want to target and answer how you believe they would. Make some educated guesses and assumptions to get started, and correct course later.

2. Google "free personality tests". There are many to choose from however its best to select a popular one with great personality profile descriptions. Select one that's not to too complicated and only has 'yes' or 'no' answers. It must be quick and easy. Give it a test drive to check you're happy with it. Work out how to print the questionnaire answers or take a screen shot prior to submitting it for the results.

3. Approach your list of great customers explaining to them that they are one of the top few customers you love working with, and that you are doing a little research so you can attract more customers just like them. Stroke their ego a little, it never hurts.

4. Request a 15-20 minute phone interview to run through a quick questionnaire which will help you create a profile of your ideal customer. Tell them it will be a bit of fun, and you can also give

them their personality profile results if they like. Reassure them there will be nothing too personal.

5. Some will agree to do it immediately while others will schedule a time. You could consider sending them a bottle of wine thanking them in advance if you wish. Some may feel uncomfortable, so reassure them that it's fine not to participate. It's not worth upsetting the relationship.

6. Prior to commencing the questionnaire explain it's a set of questions with no right or wrong answers, and that you only need a 'yes' or 'no'. Tell them in advance that their first instinctive answer is the best. Complete the questions and print or take a screenshot before submitting the data. Once that's done, tell them the result if they wish, and offer to send them the results via email.

7. Once you have completed the questionnaire for everyone on your list, collate all the answers working out how the majority responded to each question. If you have a draw on any, favour the response from the best customer on your list. It's probably not going to make a major difference anyway.

8. Fill in the questionnaire with the most popular answers, and out will pop the profile of your ideal customers. Google the results and you'll find lots of information on this type of person. Pay particular attention to how you can work with or relate to this type of person.

Not all your ideal clients will fit perfectly into the profile you've created. In fact, if you were to do a profile for yourself, you will find some information to be not right for you. That's fine, it's a general guide so you can better understand what makes your ideal customers tick.

Once you have this profile, use it when creating all your marketing to attract this type of person. If it helps you to distil all this information into a simple profile and give the personality a name, do it. Give them a gender to help you, based on the most common gender of your best customers. Write all your marketing material as if you were speaking directly to this one individual. I followed this formula when deciding my audience for this book. It certainly helped the process, writing as if I were speaking to one person (you, of course), rather than writing for a crowd.

Networking Event Blunders

Standing out from the crowd makes good business sense even to mainstream business people. I've been to many networking events over the years and often politely ask, "What is it you do?". The answers are usually vague as they stumble over their words. If you ask what makes them unique, they will often give boring clichéd responses like, "We really care," or ,"It's our customer service," or some other generic ideas. Do you do what I do when I meet these people? You politely give a caring response, but deep down you're not interested at all. I know that sounds harsh, but own up to it, you do it too, right?

Occasionally you will get the opposite to this experience. When meeting someone new at an event you ask, "What is it you do?" or, "What makes you unique?" and they give some long-winded, emotion-charged pitch, leaving you puzzled as to what they actually do. They might say, "I make people's dreams come true by showing them how to create the freedom they deserve." They want you to engage in conversation to find out more, but instead they create frustration. When I hear this kind of fluff, I give them a mental head-butt and next I ask, "Okay... but what is it that you do?" This often leads to more lengthy statements and a guessing game. "So are you a Mortgage Broker?"

Don't frustrate people in this way. Be clear on what you do, so the person you are speaking with can quickly understand what industry you're in, and then highlight what makes you unique. Present it in a conversational way that actually answers the question, "What do you do?"

Find a point of difference that matters to your ideal customers, and make it interesting. It's a process where you must create interest first before trying to make a sale. When networking, the only sale you should be trying to make is to sell yourself. Get them to know you, like you, and trust you.

Your point of difference comes from your unique standpoint and could include any number of features: location, processes, ingredients, availability etc. Can you deliver your product faster than the competition? Do you use higher quality ingredients? Are you more accessible than your competitor's? The more relevant and compelling your message is to your customers, the more interesting it will be.

Consider these questions:

- What are your target market's biggest frustrations?

- What benefits are they looking for from your product or service?

- How can you eliminate their frustrations and give them the benefits they desire?

"One of the challenges in networking is everybody thinks it's making cold calls to strangers. Actually, it's the people who already have strong trust relationships with you, who know you're dedicated, smart, and a team player, who can help you."

– Reid Hoffman

It is beneficial to have a range of short yet impressive statements about what you do, the products or services you offer, and how your customers benefit. Keep it conversational according to the connection you make with the people you're speaking with, and the amount of time you have to chat.

Like all good conversations, if you focus on the person you're talking with and how your message relates to them, they will find you more interesting. Because the people you meet may have pre-conceived ideas about your industry, emphasise your standpoint and the benefits you provide. People relate best to storytelling, so real life case studies are a great way to make a connection.

Here's a model you can use to formulate your own pitch:

You know how many *(insert your target market here)* often struggle with *(insert the problem you solve here)*?

I help people like that. For example, I've been working with *(insert person here)*. He/she came to me because he/she wanted to *(insert details of the problems solved here)*.

We worked through these issues together and as a result *(describe the outcome here)*.

I love helping people with *(insert the problem you solve here)*.

Next it's your job to get them talking to keep the connection conversational. It's not the time to start flogging your wares.

Don't copy this formula, exactly, like a robot. Adjust it so it sounds natural and sits right for you. Business related conversations are often short. Nobody likes being spoken at or 'sold to'. Using the above model often creates a meaningful connection with the person you are speaking with. It is also short enough to be delivered during a networking introduction. It can be expanded and contracted depending on the nature of the conversation that begins. It's good to have some kind of memory hook or catch that will make you interesting and cause the person to remember you.

Whatever you prepare, keep it flexible and natural sounding so you can tweak it depending on the kind of person you are talking to. For example, if you're speaking with a middle aged, professional woman and have a case study of a middle aged, professional woman you worked with, use it. Emphasise the specific benefits, or problems you fix that they may relate to.

Nonconformist

My wife Lisa smashed this out of the park recently. She is a natural networker because she is always wanting to help people and loves to relate and share stories. We were having a meeting with Margaret, a staff member at our local bank. We were there to set up accounts for a new investment property and had our daughter, Grace, with us so the conversation started out relational, based around kids. Margaret asked about our kids, and Lisa reciprocated asking about her family. Margaret explained she had two adult children who were both due to have babies soon. It was a typical, friendly conversation that I wanted to wrap up, get the paperwork done, and move on but Lisas relational skills were at work. We got started on the nitty-gritty paperwork and I was happy to move through it fast.

Margaret got to the point in the paperwork about employment and asked Lisa what her career was, and where she works. Lisa explained how she trains childcare workers, and one of the areas they cover is First-Aid specific to caring for kids. The inflection in her voice invited Margaret to find out more about it, so she did. Lisa explained how it can be part of the entire course or taken as a stand-alone short course, mentioning how grandparents often take the short course. Kids were obviously on Margaret's radar and she asked some further questions about the course. Lisa answered her questions, explaining the benefits of the course and finished up with a compelling story. There was a grandmother, she explained, who recently did the short-course wanting to be better equipped to care for her grandkids. Just two weeks after the course, the grandmother was driving her grandson home and stopped in to get some petrol. She ran in to pay with her grandson when he saw a packet of Mentos which he asked for. What grandmother can refuse their grandkids lollies? They went back out to the car and were driving home when the grandmother

> *"The entrepreneur always searches for change, responds to it, and exploits it as an opportunity."*
> **– Peter F. Drucker**

81

noticed her grandson was very quiet. She turned around and he was blue. He was choking on the Mentos! She slammed on the brakes, jumped out, and did what she was taught in the short-course, saving the boy's life.

Margaret's eyes were wide open as she engaged with the story. Right then, Margaret understood the importance of the course and would have signed up on the spot if she could have. It was the perfect pitch because it didn't sound like a pitch at all. It sounded like two people having a normal conversation. It was tailored perfectly for the recipient who immediately saw the value. Well done Lisa!

If you are new to networking and feel nervous, work out some good stories to use, something simple and compelling that links you to your target market. As you become more experienced, you can improve and adjust it. Develop your delivery over time, as you find out what works best for your business and personality. Let your passion shine through in your conversation. Your passion is what people connect with.

Eliminate Options

A common misconception is that the more options you provide your prospects, the more likely you will make a sale. This thinking comes from the belief that people, when offered choices, are more equipped to make a better decision. More often than not the exact opposite proves to be true.

Too many choices can confuse customers. Providing advice and direction on the 'best' option can make the customer feel confident in their purchase.

When you design your marketing material, focus on a small range, rather than every item you could sell. Many researchers have experimented with options and have found that 'less' is 'more'. Try a few designs featuring different products and see which one produces the best results. Your most profitable item may not bring the most customers through the door. It may be a smaller, unique product you supply that gets the customers interested, and from this position you make the larger sales.

If you currently sell widgets in 30 different colours and styles, try promoting six, hiding the others away for the purposes of the experiment. If this proves to be more successful, you could always use the other colours as 'limited editions' to clear the stock later. You could promote one at a time, thereby creating a sense of scarcity. Scarcity sells!

> *"The enemy of art is the absence of limitations."*
> **– Orson Welles**

Having a large selection may get people's attention, but often results in fewer sales. If your customers have too many choices it can overwhelm them, and in the end they won't take up the offer. If there are only a couple of options to evaluate, customers can process that information quickly and make a decision.

Experiment with your options so you discover the most profitable combination. Your website is a great place to experiment because it can be quickly and easily modified if you have a Content Management System (check out www.simplemanifesto.com/members for my current recommendations).

Try featuring a select range of popular products and eliminating others from your website temporarily to test and measure what impact this has on the sales.

Packaging v Unpackaging

Packaging is also a great way to create fewer options and greater value for your customers. If you sell a range of products that commonly go together, creating a package or series of packages (for example, Gold, Silver, and Bronze) makes the decision-making process easier for customers. When investing in something that is valuable, many people will consider buying an accessory of similar perceived value, so package it up for them in advance to make the decision simple.

On the flip-side, as a way to differentiate your business, you can 'unpackage' if your competitors are all packaging their offering. Often times when you are looking for quotes for a particular product or service, the salesperson will try to upsell you into a 'complete package'. For example, if you approach a graphic designer to create a logo, they may try to sell you an entire branding strategy. The larger the organisation, and the less hands-on the 'account manager' you're speaking with, the more likely they will try this strategy. It makes perfect sense when you understand they are sales people masquerading as 'account managers'. The account they are managing most is their bank account since they are probably incentivised by commissions.

Don't work with anyone who continually tries to put their agenda ahead of yours. Cut them loose. If your competitors are playing this game, be the nonconformist and minimise the options you present to the customer. Present them with one single, best-suited choice, and explain why they don't need all the other 'stuff' they are being offered.

Here's some contradictory advice: There is a time when adding more options can help increase your success, and it's related to packaging. When a customer is about to make an investment they are often likely to make further purchases related to that product or service. The key here is to make a match on the perceived quality and price of a product. For example, if the customer is about to purchase an expensive brand of shoes, then suggesting a set of socks with the same brand will often create more sales. If you were to promote a budget range of socks with a high-end shoe, you're likely to be less successful. The same is true if the customer was purchasing a cheap pair of shoes and you recommended your most expensive socks. This kind of upselling is possible in face-to-face sales and online shopping websites. Keep the process simple so you don't lose customers in the process.

Eliminate Features

This may sound counter-intuitive in a world constantly striving to add more, however providing less can create a distinct advantage. For years many of the elderly and tech-luddites were demanding a simple mobile phone that they could make phone calls on, nothing else. They didn't want Internet, Apps, calendars, bells and whistles. The usual response from mobile sales people, and companies producing them was, "You don't need to use all the features." That might sound like a logical response however, for this market, features meant complexity and confusion. This was the thinking of my uncle and grandmother. Even an SMS or message saying they missed a call was too much!

My uncle was having problems with his old mobile phone, so he walked to the store and bought a new "smartphone". He was so frustrated with it, he walked back to the shop to get some advice on how to work the damn thing. After much frustration, he said to the sales assistant, "If the old phone just didn't make calls when it was in my pocket it would have been perfect!" The sales assistant then realised the obvious solution.

He asked, "Sir, do you have your old mobile with you?"

"Sure," my uncle responded, pulling it out of his pocket.

The sales guy showed him how to lock and unlock the keypad preventing it from calling when bumped in his pocket. A simple solution was found and my uncle was happy. He had the mobile he wanted and the smartphone still sits at the back of a shelf somewhere never to be used again.

There are now simple mobile phones with large buttons that only call and SMS, making them easy to use. Finally a company realised they needed to remove unwanted features for a certain market segment, not tell them to ignore the unwanted features.

I had a similar experience with a potential new customer who was also a friend. She wanted an online system to manage a community based business. She needed her team to be able to record notes on members of the community, and schedule meetings so everyone was well taken care of. Her needs sounded like a perfect match to a free open-source web-based CRM (Customer Relationship Management) system I had some experience with. The CRM was jam-packed with other features not required by my friend, but easily turned off and hidden. Some of the terminology wasn't what my friend would use, however that was easily changed too. They were managing a community of members and didn't want to refer to them as customers. None of the usual sales terms typically found in CRMs were suitable, but were easily modified. I quickly installed a demo for her and arranged a meeting.

I presented this system, excited that we had found the "perfect" solution, explaining we could easily remove all the extras she didn't want, and change the wording to be suitable. I explained it could be run on their own web server so there were no additional costs. For me to customize and set it up would be only $150. In my mind the deal was done, the decision to go ahead was obvious. She needed to get approval within the organisation, which was notoriously tight even for small expenses like this. I gave her the logins to the demo so she could have a play, and show anyone she needed to.

A week or two passed and I followed up on it, but still no decision had been made. Being such a small job I left it to her to call me when she was ready to get started. Months passed by and I was curious as to what the holdup was. They had decided to go ahead with a different system. Why? They chose a system that specialised in what they do, nothing else. The system already had the wording they were familiar with in the demo. It was a simple system that did only what they wanted. It was a perfect fit for their niche. What I presented would have been an almost identical system once configured for them, but the perceived complexity and features confused them.

In the end they went with a subscription-based, software as a service system where they pay about $100 a month. That's $1200 a year, year in year out. It's likely they will continue with this system for many years to come since their data will be locked up in it. Think of what it will cost this community organisation in the long run compared to the $150 that I would have charged. I beat them easily on price, had the advantage of being trusted since it was my friend, but I still lost the deal. Why? Complexity and confusion. Sounds crazy I know but lesson learnt!

Present the solution to the problem and nothing but the solution. Cut the fat and give your niche exactly what they want. You can always add features later if your niche demands it, but don't ever confuse the sale with complexity.

Some of the features we assume our customers want, prove not to be important to them at all. I'm not much of a Gamer but I know one thing, my boys love the game,

> *"Sometimes the questions are complicated and the answers are simple."*
> **– Dr. Seuss**

Minecraft. It might be a passing fad, who knows. What I do know is right now it's incredibly popular and it defies what many thought was required to make a popular game. Most thought that having realistic graphics was one of the most important things to make a successful game. Minecraft proves these assumptions to be wrong. I don't get it, but I don't need to. The graphics are blocky and the kids love it. They play the game, wear the T-shirts, and collect anything associated with these characters.

Embrace Restraints

Don't let perceived limitations disempower you. The restraints you experience now can be reimagined to be your biggest source of creativity. You may feel restricted by a lack of money, a lack of technical know-how, or a lack of resources. We live with limitations, some physical and some mental. Your limitations only have the power to stop your business if you allow them to. There is always another way.

Consider Theodor Seuss Geisel, better known by his pen name Dr. Seuss. None of us would ever think of his writing as bland or without creativity, however he wrote with a consistent, restrictive flow. It's these restraints that gave his work an unusual quirkiness many of us love. If there wasn't a word that would fit well with the flow of his writing, he would invent one. Restraints were not a problem. Consider his work,

"Green Eggs and Ham" that was written with just 50 words as a result of a bet. Now that's creative!

I love to use quotes to inspire me, and Dr. Seuss is one of the most amazing sources of inspiration. So many gems are communicated so eloquently in his writing. Even if his books are written for children, they are always laced with life lessons, almost like a parable.

The Imperfectionist

It's not about perfection, it's about perfecting. SAs are idealists, always aiming for innovation. Don't confuse this with perfectionism. Perfect is an impossible goal, yet it's something SAs constantly aim towards realising they will never 'arrive'. I get frustrated with self-proclaimed perfectionists. They tell you like it's some kind of badge of honour. Perfectionists must either be depressed or deluded, because very few things are perfect. I'm always perfecting my work, but I am not a perfectionist. Perfectionism will kill your business before it even begins. Your business will never be perfect, your website will never be perfect, and your customers will never be perfect.

Look at it this way, John is trying to launch something new and is waiting for it to be perfect. Mary has a similar goal and launches something 80% complete, but functional. Which is more perfect, John who has nothing to show for his work or Mary who has something tangible? If Mary is an SA like you, with some loyal customers who believe in what she's trying to do, who would you bet on?

I'm not suggesting Mary should stop there. She should continue to improve what she has as she builds momentum, creates engagement with customers, and gathers feedback. John's idea of perfection is based on his assumptions, while Mary can gauge interest and feedback as she develops her business. She can move towards her customers understanding of what 'perfect' is as she builds the business. She can run a flexible and dynamic business, capitalising on opportunities as they arise, while John is limited by his own set of ideals that may not be important to his customers. Mary continues to perfect her business while John will never get started with his idea of a perfect business.

I'm not suggesting Mary shouldn't have a clearly-defined goal either. She must hold to her unique standpoint and principles for any actions she takes. Few standpoints completely restrict you, making you inflexible to adapt or change your tactics. Vision, purpose, values, principles and your standpoint will stay unchanged, but strategies, actions, and tactics will always adapt and evolve.

"Disneyland will never be completed. It will continue to grow as long as there is imagination left in the world."
– Walt Disney

Allowing yourself to be comfortable with imperfection equips you to explore new approaches without fear of failure or rejection, knowing you can always correct course and improve your business as you start to make progress. Let's explore this new approach further in the following Lens...

approach

Noun:

A way of dealing with a situation or problem.

Synonyms:

attitude, slant, perspective, point of view, viewpoint, outlook, line of attack, line of action, method, procedure, process, technique, MO, style, strategy, stratagem, way, manner, mode, tactic, tack, path, system, Modus operandi

(Credit Google.com - edited)

Okay, so you have a compelling standpoint, and you have made peace with the fact that you are a nonconformist despite the opposition it attracts. I know, I know, you probably love being nonconformist, you rebel, you! Now it's time to take this mindset and put it into practice. Let's explore some new approaches for your business through your unique perspective.

Get Stuff Done by Eliminating Tasks

Entrepreneurs are creative people who see opportunities for new products and services in response to customers' needs. The problem they face is the overwhelming number of tasks required day in, day out. Entrepreneurs and small business owners, are typically busy managing their day-to-day operations. They often can't find the time or money to invest into major business improvements.

The good news is, you don't need a huge budget to supercharge your business. You don't need hours and hours to get it done either. There are simple principles you can implement in your business today to get started fast. It's a matter of selecting what will work best for you, experimenting with it, testing it, and scaling it up once you know it works.

To get to that point you will need to be able to "see the forest for the trees," which will take good time management. I use those words reluctantly because of all the complicated "time management" systems and philosophies out there which I don't want to be associated with. However, one of the biggest traps for entrepreneurs is a lack of time, so this book couldn't avoid the topic and do justice by you. Also, I know from experience that most problems in your business will have less impact if your time management is taken care of.

Time management can be a complicated beast. There are many books about it, written by people in various fields, because time management is an issue almost everyone faces. There is no need to "reinvent the wheel", if you are following a time management system that works for you, great.

As we've already covered, you must be selective. As an entrepreneur, if you try to do everything, you'll do nothing effectively. Sometimes it's far more efficient to assign tasks to specialised people rather than attempt to complete it all yourself, even if it's a core skill of yours. We will come back to this point in Lens 4.

Business should not be about juggling an endless list of meaningless tasks. While there is a place for traditional time management strategies, it's more important to eliminate tasks from your to-do list so you can focus on your most profitable and enjoyable goals.

Set aside time in your schedule for the one big goal you are working on right now and treat it as a priority, trying new approaches to propel you forward as you go. Set yourself a due date that is tight but realistic. This will keep you focused on the most critical tasks, and minimise any fluffing around. If you find it hard to focus, make yourself accountable to friends who will pull you up if you don't meet your deadlines. A bold statement on social media might be all it takes. For example "I'm going to have my book draft written by January." I did it for the book you are reading and it certainly helped get it done. I didn't want to look like a failure. Try it for your big goal.

> *"The secret of getting ahead is getting started."*
> — **Mark Twain**

Drop any non-essential tasks and watch your productivity soar. By focusing on your big goal you will be forced to eliminate less important tasks, or find a better way to do them.

The reality is, we all struggle to eliminate tasks and focus on one goal at a time. I hope at the very least, you try to reduce some of the busywork you currently have on your to-do list. You can have multiple projects on the go at once and that keeps life interesting. Just be aware you won't reach success with any of them as fast as you will if you focus on one big goal at a time.

Being a Start-up is No Excuse!

I've heard it said that about eight in 10 Start-ups fail in their first year. I didn't bother checking this statistic because I don't really care, and we shouldn't be dictated to by statistics, or take sympathy in them. Some people seem to love misery and act like it's part of their identity.

Like you, I've got friends on Facebook who continually whinge about how hard their lives are. Yes, I want to respond, "It must really suck being you," but Lisa always curbs my naughtiness. I think it would actually do them good to hear it. It might jolt them out of the cycle of constantly being negative hoping to attract some positive encouragement. It can be a vicious cycle similar to what Jack (the ice addict) found himself in.

The same thing happens in Start-ups. The failure rate is so high that it becomes an excuse to fail. Yes, the failure rates are high, whatever they may be. That's the reality you have to deal with, but it shouldn't discourage you from starting a new business. The only thing it should discourage you from is following the common Start-up philosophies that fail in eight out of 10 businesses. Start-ups are great at thinking big, and that's great. It's a healthy approach to life and business, and this book will help you beat the odds.

Firstly, don't let the long-term big thing rob you of the short-term need for cash. The sooner you can create cash-flow, the sooner you can reinvest back into your business and build more momentum. Aim for short-term profit, and long-term sustainable growth. The typical Start-ups burn through money for far too long before they start to turn a profit, if they ever do. That's a foolish business model and one you are best to avoid.

Traditional business consultants may ask you if you want to build equity in your business, or create profit. Service-based businesses tend to be good at creating profit, but suck at building a sellable business. Product-based business tend to build equity which can make them high value if they choose to sell out. It's a crazy question when you think about it. It shouldn't be an either/or question. Build both! Create profit that will sustain you now, while you work on the longer-term goal of building a business of high value.

There are still risks. Launching any new business venture takes an element of risk, but it's about minimising those risks. Even if you were to buy a franchise with a "proven" business model there's no certainty it will work. There are too many variables. Your location will be different, the number of competitors may be different, and there are plenty of other factors outside your control that could come into play, which you didn't consider. Even if you purchase an established business with a strong track record, there are no guarantees the market conditions won't change and you probably have had to risk a whole lot more money buying the business in the first place. Buying that video store may not have been such a great decision after all.

> *"To me, if life boils down to one thing, it's movement. To live is to keep moving."*
> **– Jerry Seinfeld**

Entrepreneurs are those that take a calculated risk and launch something new and innovative. I'm not talking about mindless danger junkies, but daring risk takers who work out of their convictions. It's all about calculated risks, and about having the courage to back yourself and your ideas, regardless of how stretching they may seem. Persist, despite the criticism and even opposition of those around you. Risks come with the promise of opportunity. Taking those opportunities implies that you take with them, an element of risk. It's unavoidable. The road to success is paved with obstacles. Are you ready for the challenge?

Movements and Momentum

Conventional wisdom says the fastest way from point A to point B is a straight line, "as the crow flies" so to speak. It may be true in some cases, however I've found it's an assumption that is not always true. I've found the fastest way from point A to point B is more like ice-skating, particularly when starting something unique. While taking off, you need to push a little sideways to create some friction to propel you forward. You head off in the general direction, correcting course as you go and not a straight line. As momentum is gathered and you reach maximum speed, then gliding across the ice in a straight line is possible. If you tried travelling in a straight line from the start you would never create the momentum to reach the destination. There simply wouldn't be enough friction to push off from.

In the early stages of a new business or a new venture within your business, friction is not only expected, it's required. You'll get feedback in the early stages that you can act on and move forward from. You keep your eye on the end goal (Point B), but you move side-to-side, making adjustments throughout the process. As you get faster, you begin to travel straighter until you reach the maximum speed that you can handle. Then you glide on to point B in a straight line. It's a process that all fast growth businesses go through.

Momentum is created in the same way ice-skaters create accelerated movement. You can easily become an information junkie, running from seminar to seminar, buying resource after resource looking for the secret formula that will take you from point A to point B fast. The trouble is, what you are looking for probably doesn't exist – not in the format you are looking for anyway. You may have been looking for a "straight line" system, but the real solution is to change your mindset. To think more like the ice-skater who get's down low, pushing from side to side as acceleration in gathered. Only when they reach a high speed do they begin to gracefully glide to the final destination.

Branding Lies & Logo Design

Let's get skating: chances are some of you are going to experience some friction in this chapter, so hear me out. We will use a bit of friction at the start to glide through to the end goal, so hear me out. Just like it takes a mindset shift to take you from point A to point B fast, it takes another mindset shift when it comes to branding, and what it actually means to you and your business. If you've been fed misinformation about what branding is for long enough what I'm about to say may sound counter-intuitive, even heretical if you are a 'branding expert'. It's my conviction that many marketing gurus have got it wrong. They've taken what should be simple, and complicated it, making it a big consulting business full of lofty ideas. Here's the truth. The term branding comes from the age-old practice of using a hot iron to mark livestock to identify ownership. The graphic created by this process acted much like a logo does today, helping to identify and differentiate a product or service. An animal that hasn't been branded is called a 'slick'. There are many branding experts spruiking that a brand is not a logo, don't let their slick semantics confuse you.

Don't ever let marketing guru's complicate business for you, particularly when they get started on branding. If you read, watch, or listen to other resources about branding, you'll need to understand where they are coming from. They'll package up a whole lot of ideas as branding, so filter out the rhetoric, spit out the bones, and digest the good parts of what they might be saying.

To make it crystal clear for you, your business name and logo are the most significant aspects of your branding. Don't be persuaded otherwise. When I speak of branding I'm primarily speaking about your logo and the support graphics that accompany it. It's that simple.

Rant over! Now lets glide through the following simple branding principles...

Logos communicate complex concepts and ideas through simplified images and typefaces that distinctively and effectively express a desired message. The thinking behind a logo is the true art of logo design. I'm sure you've noticed some logos are clever and effective, while other logos fail to represent the company's message well. The latter is usually due to lazy thinking and poor design. I'm not saying you need to come up with an eight-page rationale, but if your logo is going to stand the test of time, it needs to be well thought out.

Your logo should symbolise, in a distinct way, what your business is about and what it stands for. Your logo design is a visual representation to the world, of who you are as a business. A tired, unimaginative, dime-a-dozen logo design reflects a tired, unimaginative, dime-a-dozen business. You want your logo to reflect your unique standpoint and speak to your customers about your credibility, experience and trustworthiness.

When having a logo designed, you should consider your:

- Standpoint

- Vision

- Culture

- Personality

- Values

- Point of difference

- Target market

Your logo design is an artistic, creative representation of your business that is subject to opinion and personal preferences. Logo design is an artistic representation, and we all interpret art differently. Your logo design must communicate effectively to your target market. It's just a bonus if you, as the business owner, like it.

Your personal preferences matter less than the preferences of your target market. Don't dictate the design style based on your own personal preferences alone. Listen to the thoughts and opinions of others, particularly those who fit within your target market or an experienced designer who has the expertise and insight to know what works.

The purpose of a logo is to identify and represent a business or a product range within a business. An effective logo should be instantly recognisable and create a lasting impression. Do not over-complicate the image that you are creating in your customer's minds with too many messages, ideas, and clutter. Create a simple eye-catching visual message, and repeat it over and over again until it sticks in the minds of your target market. Don't worry about them getting sick of it. You will get sick of it long before they do, so stick with it.

Unless you are a professional graphic designer, logo design isn't something you should attempt yourself. Get a designer who has an eye for creativity and an understanding of your business. This kind of know-how is not something you can achieve with generic logo design templates.

Never use a template logo design or clipart. There are a huge number of possible templates to select from these days, however the risks are not worth it. When you don't have an original logo design, you don't hold exclusive rights to use it. This gives you no control over who else uses the same design. Go with a template or clip-art and you could end up with a logo that is exactly the same as someone else in your local community. Worse still, it could be your direct competitor. They could even use it for deceptive purposes, leaving you helpless when it comes to protecting your identity. You will not have a distinctive identity for your business, and run the risk of being associated with others using the same design.

Your logo should be both original and attractive to your target market. A unique logo should get your business noticed for the right reasons. It should become one of your most prominent and valuable assets. A well-designed, original logo can be an effective way to communicate what makes you unique as a business, and what it is that sets you apart from the competition.

Often businesses get to a point where they realise the logo they have been using is not doing them justice. Consider the long-term value of your business and spend a few extra bucks to get your logo designed right the first time. Avoid shortcuts that may create

> *"There was no one near to confuse me, so I was forced to become original."*
> **– Joseph Haydn**

complications as the business expands and matures. Get professional help. A good designer can help you clarify your thoughts and make suggestions on what design elements are going to be most effective. They will help you get the most out of your logo design budget, and provide a finished product that works hard for your business, for years to come.

If you're starting a new business, your graphic designer can create an entirely new logo from the ground up. If you are already in business and have a logo you are not entirely happy with, it may simply be a matter of redesigning and reinvigorating your current design.

Changing your logo can be an expensive and complicated process. Not so much for the logo design itself, the biggest cost is often replacing your logo everywhere it has been used. You may need to reprint new business cards, stationery, promotional items, update your website, signage, ads, and social media accounts. The list goes on and on. It's much better to spend the time and effort to get your logo designed well the first time. While other aspects of your business can adapt and evolve easily, your logo should remain consistent where-ever possible. "Measure twice and cut once".

Get your finished logo files in a variety of formats so you can use it for any purpose in the future, and ensure you own the Intellectual Property. An originally created logo is subject to copyright, so ensure your logo designer provides you with this copyright once the job is complete. Just because you commissioned a logo design project, does not mean you own the Intellectual Property. Get the copyright and if you want to take it to the next level, get it trademarked. Many branding and design agencies won't be completely transparent about this and end up holding you at ransom over your logo design. I've seen companies cough up more and more cash every time they need to use their logo in a new way.

Simplify your logo design. Let the great logos of big brands inspire you. They often spend a fortune on it, and almost always select a simple, crisp, clean design. You don't need to spend what they do to end up with a similar result. Small businesses often try to say too much within their logo. The result is an ineffective, unclear message that looks cheap and nasty.

Don't imitate any other logo. Let other logos inspire you, but make yours unique. Be bold. A provocative, cheeky logo can get attention. Show your business personality. In a marketplace packed with competitors selling similar products or services, use your logo to create a distinctive image. Think about companies you know with iconic brands. What makes their logo remarkable?

Select fonts, colours, and styles that are timeless. Your logo isn't something you want to update regularly, so go with something that will last. Your logo should be distinctive yet sophisticated and simple.

Try not to make your logo either too wide or too tall. You will often have size restrictions and requirements when using your logo, so it needs to be suitable for a range of applications. You may choose to have horizontal and vertical versions of your logo to give you more flexibility.

While the visual appeal of your logo is important, you should also consider functionality. It must be useable in all kinds of environments. It must also be instantly recognisable, whether it is stamped on an envelope or scaled up to a large billboard. Use clean and legible typography that won't become out-dated quickly.

Consider what the logo will look like at different sizes and in different situations to ensure it remains legible and effective. Test the quality of the logo with a black and white version.

Create a logo that will withstand the changes and developments in your business. Don't put your top product into your logo. In a few years you might be selling something completely different.

How much should you spend on logo design? Some pay a few bucks, some pay thousands, and some have even paid millions. The truth is, the million-dollar logo isn't necessarily any better than one that cost a few hundred dollars. The million-dollar logo has probably been designed by 'committee' since so much is at stake. It's often a complete waste of resources. You don't want to pay too little either. It's not something you want to get wrong. I can't tell you what to spend on your logo design, but I am saying you should consider it an investment for your long-term business success. Your logo will be used in a huge range of places across advertising, marketing, and corporate communications. When a business has a poor quality logo design, it makes it tough for many of your future marketing endeavours since it's hard to camouflage a terrible logo.

While you can manage your own logo designing process, it's helpful to get external perspectives from others. Sometimes we get so close to our own businesses that we miss what others can see quickly and easily.

What You Don't Know Can Hurt You

As an SA, you are probably a big picture person with a dream. We are about to get stuck into website design and development, which is a lot of fun, but there's some technical stuff that we must cover first. It's not possible to teach you all the technical aspects of web development in this book, nor should you want me to. I know it can be boring but it's important to cover this, because getting it wrong can cost your business big time.

You don't need to get bogged down with all the technicalities of coding, however you do need to be aware that what you don't know can hurt your website performance. You are not expected to know coding languages and how it all works, you just have to know if it is working. It's like my car. Most days I jump into my car, start the engine, and drive to the office. I don't ever consider how the mechanics work and what is happening behind the scenes, until something is wrong. If an odd noise develops in my car or something else seems to be a problem, that's the only time I would think about what makes my car run. The same is true with websites. Often a website is built and it looks great on one browser, but it doesn't run well on other browsers, PC monitors, and devices. What do search engines see when they visit your website? When tested, many websites show coding errors the owner is unaware of, and that could be causing massive problems.

I'm often called in to fix these broken websites, which usually stem from simple errors.

With poor quality coding, the three biggest risks you face are:

"It is well for the heart to be naive and the mind not to be."

– Anatole France

1. Your website appearing incorrectly to some visitors (in some cases it's not even usable).

2. Search engines are giving you little traffic (in some cases they won't index the website at all).

3. Your website is slow loading making a terrible user experience.

That's the bad news. The good news is, they are often easy to fix. Often a few small changes can have a massive impact on your overall website performance. This is why it is worth investing in a professional web developer, who avoids these mistakes while you focus on building your business.

It takes technical know-how, creative skills, and marketing experience to know what works. Select a developer you can trust and who knows what they are doing. Select someone who is goal-driven in creating your website. Your most important online presence is your website. It's where you can showcase your professionalism and have full creative control. No social media platform can rival this so I encourage you to pay close attention to who you select to build it. Don't get overwhelmed with all the possibilities either, a good web developer will get your website online fast with the goal of further enhancing and improving it as your business develops and your budget allows. Think back to the imperfections faced by Mary and how she developed her business over time as she got feedback and gained momentum. Websites are flexible, dynamic, and easily adapt and evolve, so use that to your advantage. If you can only afford a basic website right now, get it launched with the intention to expand and improve it as you make progress.

Okay now for the fun stuff...

Simple Website Marketing

First impressions count. You only have seconds to capture the interest of your website visitors, and if you're a Start-up, you might only have one chance, when your prospect takes a look. It's difficult to communicate a message through the text on your website alone in this time. It's great to have compelling information on your website. If your website design puts visitors off before they have read a word, you're leaving money on the table.

Your online presence is often the public face of your business. Websites are often the first opportunity for prospects to learn more about a business before purchasing. You need a web design that's user-friendly, attractive, easy to navigate, and meets your business agenda.

Almost every person I meet has some area of their website that they are not completely happy with. They may be attracting lots of traffic, but not enough of it converts into sales. They may love the design, but the content isn't clear. Maybe the website is not working so well on some devices. While most web developers will pitch to you a complete new package, this is often not in your best interest. Good websites adapt and evolve over time as the business develops and new opportunities are explored. It's not like print-based marketing material where once a project is complete, you live with it until you finish the print run. Websites are flexible, dynamic and can be tinkered with regularly. They are never finished.

This is where an SA's mindset is invaluable – you can adapt faster than your competitors and respond to customers needs. Your website should be seen as an ongoing investment, not a once-off expense. A good website will produce profit for your business, and as you improve it your profit should also increase. Many businesses don't make the most out of their website because they believe it's a complicated, expensive process. This can be true if you hire the wrong web developer, or worse still, try to do it yourself.

Your website visitors assess your professionalism through your website. They want to be assured they are dealing with a reputable business. Your business name and logo needs to be a prominent fixture on each and every webpage. This gives users the feeling that the business is proud of who they are, and creates a sense of integrity.

Take your target market into consideration when choosing the right colours for your website. Use the colours from your logo design and potentially one or two additional colours to draw attention to important areas of the website. Less is more when it comes to colours. It is often best if you opt for a two or three-toned website. These colours are usually determined by your logo. The colours you use on your website should also be used throughout your marketing material to create consistency. It's not about selecting your favourite colours, it's about the business objectives.

Great websites evolve over time, so get started. Make short and long-term goals for your website, and provide this information to your web developer. With this knowledge they may be able to make recommendations to help you achieve your goals in efficient ways you may not have considered.

> *"Good design is a lot like clear thinking made visual."*
> **– Edward Tufte**

When your web developer understands where you are headed, they can design and structure your website so it will accommodate your future requirements. For example, if you plan to add more items to your website menu at a later stage, the developer can keep this in mind and create a menu structure that can be easily added to without running out of space.

Almost every website I've ever worked on includes one or more of these goals:

- To generate new sales or leads

- To establish a connection with a chosen target market

- To grow an opt-in subscription list

- To improve communications with customers and prospects

While a short-term goal for your website may simply be to get an online presence, consider your long-term goals so you won't need to start again from scratch. This will save you time and money in the long run.

Before you start developing your website, research the competition. This does not mean you should copy what they are doing. You should also visit the websites of complementary businesses, and even completely different businesses. Remember the SA is always looking to learn and this can be a goldmine of ideas that you could introduce to your industry. Jot down any websites of interest so you can easily brief your web developer using these examples.

If you have prepared a clear brief, a good web developer will be able to make suggestions and recommendations to enhance the final outcome. They will take your vision for the structure and content, and create a unique design to meet your specific needs.

It will help if you tell web developers your budget when they are preparing your proposal. A lot of people try to avoid sharing their budget thinking the developer will try and get them to spend all of it rather than provide the best possible price. While this may be true of some developers, knowing the budget will help them make suitable recommendations as they know where you sit financially. For example, if the budget is tight, the developer may be able to recommend existing templates or themes that can be used instead of custom creating your web design from the ground up. While this approach may not be the perfect fit for what you had in mind, it may be the best possible option based on your financial restraints. They won't know to make these recommendations if they don't know what your budget is. The budget for your website may also determine what features you can include now, and what you introduce at a later stage. Your budget may dictate which web developers you consider approaching. There are large digital agencies that don't do anything for less than $10,000, and there are others who can produce basic websites for a few hundred dollars. Regardless of what your budget is, being specific and transparent about your plans and budget will help you get the best possible advice and results.

Once you have briefed your web developer, ensure they understand you are open to recommendations and suggestions. Stay flexible. You don't know what you don't know, and you should be willing to take guidance from anyone, particularly people you are paying! Your developer should be in touch with the latest trends and capabilities that you may not be aware of. Arrange a meeting with your developer, so you can go over the brief and further develop your plans together. This will give you the chance to clarify details and ensure that you're both on the same page. Throughout this discussion, your developer will likely ask questions about things your never even considered and your brief will evolve into a fully-developed, website strategy.

There are many website options available that should be avoided. These are strategies that cost you time and money with no proven results, or strategies that are too technical and confusing for non-techies. Too often these strategies become a distraction. Your website strategy should be clear and simple, with a minimal amount of time or money invested so you can test, measure, and tweak it, ensuring it produces results.

Make your website the mother-ship of your marketing. Whether it be social media marketing or some form of print based marketing, drive all marketing through your website where people can easily respond to your offers and get further information. You control the messages within your own website and can minimise distractions that the visitor cannot avoid in other environments.

Complicated navigation is a deal breaker

Here's a simple law to live by online: If people can't find what they're looking for on your website fast, they will leave. Structure and design your website in a way that allows easy navigation now, and in the future, as you add products or services. There may be a small additional cost involved in developing your website to be future-ready, however you will save on the cost of updates later. Plan your website framework. Sounds technical, but it doesn't need to be. All you need is a pen and paper and start scribbling down how your website will flow. For those who prefer to do it on a PC or tablet, you could use a simple document or a spreadsheet, so you can map out the pages and navigation you want included. A more complicated diagram may be required for large-scale websites, but for most businesses this is overkill.

Mistakes in website creation can be expensive and time consuming to fix, so it is better to take the time to map out the structure of your website in advance. Focus on what the outcome should be. Leave the technical jargon to your developer.

Simple and user-friendly navigation prevents confusion and allows people to quickly find the information they are looking for. Structure your website content and navigation in the most logical sequence possible. That means logical for your customers or the industry you are targeting. Research what your competitors are doing to identify what your client's expectations may be.

Make your website functional, dynamic, and interactive, but never at the expense of simplicity. Apply the KISS or "Keep it Simple, Stupid" principle. The functionality of your website should not frustrate your visitors. Use easy-to-use buttons and menus across all devices. Visitors won't waste time trying to work out how to navigate through your website. Don't let your love for anything that's shiny and moves, get the better of you. While using some animation may catch the attention of your visitors, overdoing it is likely to drive them away.

If you're going to have a large website with lots of content, include a search box so visitors can easily find what they're looking for. If you have lengthy pages, you could include a menu in the footer or a button to take visitors back to the top of the page.

I love unconventional thinking, testing assumptions, and breaking rules, however I don't believe your website configuration is the place to do it. Consistent, common ways of interacting online have been developed over the years, and people have learnt to follow them. If you want to break the basic rules of learnt behaviour then you should have a good reason for doing so. If you do break or bend any of the usual standards, consider usability and make it obvious how people should interact with your site.

> *"A company shouldn't get addicted to being shiny, because shiny doesn't last."*
> **– Jeff Bezos**

Use common positioning of web elements. Never chop and change the positioning of elements in your website from page to page. It's not the time to get tricky. It's a website, not a 'Where's Wally?' book! The last thing you want to do is confuse your visitors when they are interacting with your website. Make a designated place for every item so it is easy for the user to navigate. Your menu must stay in the same place. Whether it's at the top or side, it doesn't matter, so long as it is easy to find and use.

Turnkey Templates

If you're looking to get up and running fast, at low cost, using an existing template may be the best option for you. There are a number of templates and design themes available. There are web developers who use templates, but sell them as if they were custom created designs. Be careful not to be sucked in by these dodgy developers. If you're getting a pre-designed template the costs should be appropriate.

Ideally for the benefit of your business, you should create a consistent look and feel throughout all your offline and online marketing materials, and that can be compromised when using an existing template. However, to custom create your design is not always practical or viable, so templates are a perfectly acceptable starting point. You can always adapt and evolve the design later.

There are well-coded, good looking templates available and there are some terrible options. Some come at a small cost and others are free. Check www.simplemanifesto.com/members for up-to-date suggestions.

Interactivity

Be selective about what interactivity you use. Creating interactivity is now quicker, easier, and more cost effective than years gone by, but that doesn't mean you should use every bell and whistle available. There is now a range of existing 'plug-n-play' solutions that can be used and newbies often go overboard. Ask yourself, "Is it suitable for my target market?"

For example, a younger, more technical audience can cope with far more interactivity than an older, non-technical market. Even when you are targeting a young, tech-savvy market, you shouldn't go overboard with complex interactivity. People are in a hurry online, so make it simple. Remember the rule: If people can't find what they are looking for, they leave.

Balance form and function. The design should be attractive, intuitive, and user-friendly. Don't cram every inch of space with content. The overall appearance and quality of your design can be enhanced by providing some clear, white space. Less is best. There was a time when website owners would fill their website with lots of junk articles and blog posts with the view that the search engines would send them more traffic. Think about it, if your content is rubbish, all the traffic in the world won't convert into sales.

The headline "Welcome to Our Website" is a bad idea. Visitors don't always land on your homepage first anyway. They might find an article first and then click through to your homepage. It doesn't really make sense to welcome them then, does it? Once your webpage does open, if the information you present isn't clear, the user isn't going to keep reading. If they need to hunt through your site to look for the information they want, they are going to skip to a different site that will present the information in a clear, engaging manner.

Web developers are learning that simpler and lighter websites perform best, even when they are huge and have many pages. Avoid clutter. Visitors need to get your message quickly. Website design should be functional and creative without too much "congestion" and noise. While the end user experience and interaction should be simple and intuitive, what happens behind the scenes can be complex. Let simplicity rise to the forefront while complexity works behind the scenes. Focus on user-centric design. Most people use the Internet as a means of finding information and expect nearly instantaneous results. If your page is slow to load, they will look elsewhere. A few seconds is all you have for your web design to make a good first impression. Keep your website light, simple, and fast-loading. Some websites by their very nature take a long time to load, usually giving the user ample time to close the page and continue their search elsewhere. Cut back unnecessary graphic elements and sections that nobody bothers with anyway. It will make your website lighter, and help it load faster.

Does your site suffer from illegible text or a poorly selected font? Often the most effective web design improvements are not related to graphics, the logo, or the colour scheme, but on the way your text is presented. Improving the fonts and the formatting can vastly improve a website.

Typography plays a huge role in your website's legibility. Consider the font size and colours, and how they may appear on a range of devices including mobile phones and old, poor quality PC's. Don't use small-sized fonts that may strain your visitor's eyes. While it might appear fine on your screen and with your eyesight, what about people with poor quality monitors or poor vision? It must be easy to follow and read, so select a crisp font designed for easy reading. Don't overdo it with fancy fonts. Clean and simple works best. If you do choose to use a fancy font, don't use it for all your content. I'm not suggesting your fonts should be boring. You can use fancy fonts for headings or areas you want to draw attention to, for example, a handwritten style call-to-action. Balance the fancy fonts with simple, easy-reading fonts that generally look more sophisticated and under-stated. For details on web fonts that we recommend visit www.simplemanifesto.com/members

From a legibility standpoint, paragraphs should be left aligned. It's much easier to read left aligned text than centred or right aligned text particularly on small monitors or mobile devices where scrolling is involved. Centred and right aligned text can look great, but should only be used in small doses.

Don't Flash

Flash is web animation software that was popular years ago. There is better animation technology available these days so Flash should not be required. It has gradually faded away over the years since it doesn't work on iPad and iPhone, is often slow loading, and terrible for Search Engine Optimisation (SEO). We'll look at this closer in a later chapter.

Mobile Devices

It is common knowledge that a growing number of people are using mobile phones to find products and services or to research their options. Be where the action is. Your website should be responsive so it looks great on all devices (PC, tablet, and phones etc.). A responsive website "responds" to the screen size, reshaping the layout so it's appropriate for the device.

Mobile users are taking over the Internet. Mobile technology is an evolution in progress. We're still inventing fresh ways to do life "on the fly". You must make your website mobile friendly if you want to maximise your effectiveness online. It's not an option anymore!

There is now a tendency to search and shop on the go. Consider this... Jim enters the local TV shop looking for the latest, massive flat-screen TV. After speaking with the sales assistant to get some recommendations, he settles on a model he loves. It's a significant investment for Jim so he feels the need to shop around. Jim wanders off to a quiet corner in the store and discretely pulls out his mobile phone for a quick search. Jim finds the exact same model, in stock and 10% cheaper online. Jim has already been sold on the model thanks to the helpful sales assistant, however they lose the sale to the business that's 10% cheaper online.

In many ways, the future of web technology is mobile based. Mobile devices now dominate the marketplace. If you want your business to succeed online, ensure your business website can be accessed and utilised easily by phones.

Say Cheese – I must be lactose intolerant

Enough with the cheesy stock looking images please! It is quick, easy, and cheap to get your hands on stock photography these days. I recommend these images to clients all the time but I do suggest being selective. Your photographs should not look too generic. Of course it's best if you can afford the time and money to hire a professional photographer to take unique images for you. It sometimes puzzles me what they come up with. I recently had a client hire a photographer for new shots for their website and what they supplied may as well have been stock imagery. It was in that usual stocky format with cheesy poses of people who obviously had too much make-up on… and that was just the men. If you're going to use a photographer, think of something unique and creative that is specific to your business. As an SA, use your creativity to build images that connect with your target market, this will immediately distance you from the conventional corporate style photography. Often times, photographers are waiting to let their creative juices flow but are restricted by the corporate norms. Pick their

"An iPod, a phone, an internet mobile communicator… these are NOT three separate devices! And we are calling it iPhone! Today Apple is going to reinvent the phone. And here it is."

– Steve Jobs

brains and see what they can come up with creatively to make you stand out. An eye-catching image not only gets your message read, if it is interesting and unique people will also share it online.

There are free stock images available, however they tend to be medium-to-low quality photos that are not recommended for use on a professional website. You should use only high-quality images. Another thing to consider is the popularity of the stock photos. Great free stock images tend to be used across the web by many websites. Do you want your website to feature an image that one of your competitors has already used?

The more relevant and specific to your business the images are, the better. With a little Photoshop work you could adjust an image to be more suitable for your business. For example, you could add a local, recognisable background to a shot to give the impression the photo was taken locally, not somewhere overseas.

The web is full of stock image providers that can supply images for your website. Visit www.simplemanifesto.com/members for current recommendations.

Is your website message compelling?

Design your website to grab attention quickly and then entice visitors to respond to your call-to-action. Every business has their own set of goals and objectives. Your desired response may be to get visitors to buy a product or service on the spot, call your phone number, sign up to your Newsletter, chat to you online, or download your e-book, among many other options.

Are you trying to sell something? Are you trying to develop a relationship? A website can be purely informative, providing resources that visitors can browse at their leisure when they need them and then leave. It's fine to do this, however it's better to include a call-to-action if you want to grow your business. Your call-to-action must be obvious and the web design should be structured to highlight and reinforce it.

Don't use too many calls-to-action on one page. Along with being a poor marketing strategy, it will also make the design look cheap and nasty. If you want people to take action on your website, you need a clearly defined goal for each of your pages. Consider the purpose of each page in your website.

It's not "All About Search Engine Optimisation (SEO)". You only have one real chance to create a good first impression. This is very true online. While SEO for generating traffic is helpful, what that traffic does when it reaches your website is more important. As important as SEO may be to the success of your business, having a web design that attracts and engages your target market is most important.

Re-work, or ditch it and start again?

Is it better to re-work your website or to create a new one? I don't know, you tell me. It will depend on the current state of your website and your budget. Often a complete redesign is not required. Sometimes simple, yet effective changes in a website can have a significant impact on its profit-pulling potential. Some web designers may try to persuade you to do a complete new design when it's not the most critical area of your business that needs attention right now. A complete new website may only help one companies bottom-line... and it isn't yours.

You don't have to spend thousands on web design or graphic design to make your website awesome. You don't even need to hire big advertising or marketing agencies to come up with killer concepts and stunning visuals. The Internet is constantly evolving, however the fundamentals remain constant. Review your website, and if you only find a few issues, you should re-work. If there are many issues, it may be better to start again.

Experiment

You can try ideas quicker and easier online than you can with printed, mail out material, so use that to your advantage. Here are 4 potential additions for your website that you can experiment with:

1. **Add a section for testimonials.** Make the testimonials more credible by providing the full name of the people providing them (if you have their permission), as well as their website link if that's relevant. You can also embed YouTube testimonials throughout your website to engage more prospects.

2. **Create an FAQ page** that asks and answers the essential questions your customers are likely to ask before purchasing your product. It's also a great way of highlighting what your prospects should be asking your competitors, so you can showcase your competitive advantage.

3. **Add a contact form** that customers can use to request a quote or get more information. Many of your website visitors may be viewing outside business hours, so they need an easy way to connect with you. Expecting them to call in the morning doesn't cut it.

4. **Include the story of your company** in an "Our Story" section. If you have an interesting story, why not boast about it? Not everybody cares about your history but some do. They're information-hungry and want to know everything about you before making a transaction.

Landing Page Experiments

Here's something that's counter-intuitive. A simple, one page website or a landing page may prove to be more effective for your business than a fully-fledged, multi-page website. I know it doesn't easily lend itself to the content marketing strategy highlighted in a later chapter. Remember, this book isn't a step-by-step system, it's about hand picking what's most aligned with your business agenda.

Creating a compelling offer for your target market is the goal. Not all design styles suit all types of businesses and not all website structures do either. Some people are information-hungry while some prefer to stick with the basic details. Take a look at the Personality Profile of your ideal customers (as we have discussed previously) and make an intuitive decision about what the majority would prefer. Also consider your own personality and value system to make a decision on what best suits you.

What motivates and inspires your ideal customers? If you choose to use landing pages, the temptation is to cram information about all your products and services on the page. This will cause confusion. Visitors simply are not going to read all that guff. Laser-focus your message to your ideal customers only. Focus on the people who are the perfect fit for your business. Use your landing page to position yourself as a specialist with a specific customer in mind. There is no reason why you can't have a range of landing pages targeting different products and services. In fact, that should be the end goal; but start with one, experiment with it, and use what you learn for future landing pages.

"Some people remaster their records six, seven times, remix it three, four times, spend a million hours, then they always go back and hear a demo of it and they'll say, 'Aw that sounds so much better than the final mix."

– Jack White

What is the one thing you want your visitors to do once they have visited your landing page? What you are offering should guide your design style. Everything on your landing page should be about getting visitors to respond to your offer. There must be compelling reasons for them to respond. People don't visit your landing page to be impressed by flowery language. Be articulate, but don't complicate the purpose of your landing page i.e. to get a response. They are not going to contact you to find out exactly what you mean, and they don't want to feel stupid by having to ask questions. If visitors don't easily 'get it', they'll go elsewhere.

Give your visitors something of perceived value that they can receive immediately if possible. This could be a free white paper, e-book, or a video. Providing useful, educational resources is the perfect way to give your visitors immediate gratification. It's also the perfect way to expand your influence and establish yourself as a thought leader in your industry.

Your visitors are probably looking at your landing page because they have a particular need or desire that you may be able to help them with; and you have a few seconds to convince them you can deliver. Giving them something that takes them one step closer to what they are wanting is a win/win. Don't be a beggar, you are doing them a favour. They give you their contact details, you give them valuable information for free. It's a fair deal.

While you can use scare tactics to engage people's interest, you don't want them to be scared of you. It's worth including a clear Privacy Policy link on the footer of your landing page. This should make it clear how you plan to use any information you're given, and who else will have access to it. Don't use the word SPAM anywhere near your opt-in form. Have nothing like "We will never sell your information or SPAM you". That kind of text will scare people away. They shouldn't be thinking of SPAM or the emails they will be getting from you at this point. They should only be thinking of the offer you are making, and how it will help them. Engage your prospects by keeping it positive.

Audio and video on landing pages allows you to speak directly to your visitor, thereby reducing the 'stranger' factor. Your visitors can see and hear they are dealing with a real person, not some robot or cold, hard corporation. You are able to start building rapport there and then, without even meeting your potential customer. However, you should still use well-crafted copy for the script and you should present it in a natural voice. It's the human element that engages visitors.

Make it easy to share your offer. Once someone has taken up your offer, prompt them to tell their friends via social media. You could have social media sharing buttons on the thank you page. They have been given something free, so the happy juices are flowing and they may feel inclined to tell their buddies.

Landing Page Experiments – Checklist

If you already have a landing page and want to improve it, these questions should prove to be useful. Likewise, if you haven't started your landing pages you should keep these ideas in mind.

- Is the design uncluttered and simple to follow?
- Is there a compelling message 'above the fold' (on screen without scrolling)?
- Does your message clearly explain the value?
- Does it highlight why your offer is different and important?
- Does your call-to-action highlight the benefits of doing business with you or using your product?
- Is the content easy to skim read and understand?
- Does it look great on all devices? (mobile, table, PC, Mac etc.)
- Does it convey trustworthiness? (clue: if the design is poor, it won't)
- Does the layout guide the visitor's eye through to the most important messages?
- Does it communicate the quality and value of your offer?
- Does the message of your traffic-generating advertising (i.e. PPC Campaign) match the message on your landing page?
- Does the visual design of your traffic generating advertising (i.e.

Flyer or banner ad) match the design of your landing page?

- Does the webpage design 'feel' right? (i.e. Is it visually appealing?)

- Is the webpage design congruent with your values?

- Does the message motivate your target market to respond?

- Is it quick and easy for your visitors to respond impulsively to your offer?

- Is there immediate gratification for your visitors if they do respond?

A landing page that is professionally designed, attractive, looks trustworthy, and is consistent with any other marketing material used has a far better chance of turning more visitors into customers. Here are a few ideas you can experiment with to improve your landing page performance:

- **Use a short and concise headline that attracts attention.** Simplify it by stripping out any unnecessary words. Use your main keywords in it when possible, but not at the expense of a strong message.

- **Present your main points in bullet form**, preferably using a font that stands out. Use facts, but focus on the benefits for the customer.

- **Use a high-quality video.** Videos on a landing page often increase conversions. This is not surprising since it's easier for visitors to watch a video than to read your information. Videos also give you the opportunity to build trust with customers by featuring a friendly person from your business. (Normal you, the SA, is the best option). Videos should be short and punchy in the same way TV commercials are.

- **Use only one call-to-action per landing page.** Having multiple calls-to-action on your landing page can confuse visitors, who will not know what to do first, and as a result may end up doing nothing at all.

- **Include testimonials.** Whether they are short videos, reviews, or quotes from happy customers, testimonials help visitors trust your business and as a result, respond.

- **You can also increase the trust of the page** by featuring partner logos and any other third-party endorsements relevant to your business.

The Measuring Myths

With a landing page, there are only a few key metrics that you need to monitor to understand how successful it is:

- Unique Visitors

- Conversion Rate

- Traffic Sources

- Cost per Acquisition

You can experiment with options and split test everything, however these are the four key metrics to watch. Don't let anyone complicate it for you. If you don't want to get bogged down with the technical data, that's great, delegate it to someone you can trust who will synthesise the information down into something more meaningful. More on delegating tasks in Lens 4.

Unique Visitors is the first metric you should understand. Find out how many unique visitors you are attracting so you can calculate your conversion rate. With a landing page, there probably isn't much reason for them to come back and revisit frequently, so you need them to respond immediately.

"Experts often possess more data than judgment."
– Colin Powell

The **Conversion Rate** should be easy to calculate if the call-to-action requires filling in a form or making a purchase online. Simply divide the number of responses by your unique visitors and you will get your conversion rate. Your web developers should be able to put this in place for you. It can be more difficult to track if you are asking them to phone you. If this is the case, you will need a method to track the calls. If you are not getting a large number of people responding, this may be a manual process of tracking calls. It's always a good idea to ask, "What prompted you to call today?" If you're dealing with large numbers of people responding, there are fancy call tracking tools you can consider.

It's worthwhile understanding your **traffic sources** by looking at where your visitors came from. Did they click through PPC (Pay Per Click) or was it via social media? Maybe some other advertising method like direct response mail was used? You may need to make some educated guesses to work out what prompted them to visit your website. For example, if you saw a massive spike in visitors after a newspaper ad, you can be fairly confident it was the cause.

Understanding where your traffic comes from will show you what marketing methods are most beneficial, and you can eliminate or improve what's not working. Experience in online marketing will give you some intuitive clues so that you are likely to produce better results sooner. If you don't have much experience, ask someone who does.

Cost per Acquisition. If you track your conversion rate for each traffic source, and measure what you spend on the various campaigns, you can calculate how much it costs your business to generate a new lead or sale.

Pay-per-click advertising (PPC) like Google Adwords has features to make this easy, and you can drill down to what keyword and what ad is most successful. For other traffic sources, it may be more difficult. For example, social media may be free in terms of dollars spent, but it's not free in terms of time spent. If you put a dollar value on your time, you will be able to calculate the true cost per acquisition based on that figure.

Search Engine Optimisation (SEO) and Landing Pages – Good luck with that

It can be difficult to get a one-page website, like a landing page, to rank highly in search engines. Search Engine Optimisation may not be the best way to attract visitors to this type of website. You may be able to rank for the product name, obscure 'long-tail' keywords, or the words in the domain name, but that's probably going to bring in little traffic at best. More on SEO later.

The options for generating traffic to your website are endless. There is social media or blogging, for example. Maybe you can drive visitors to the landing page through offline advertising, or maybe it's as simple as people seeing your website printed on your business card. Email campaigns are also a fantastic strategy when done well. Whatever your method of attracting traffic, the same principles apply. Keep the advertising in close connection with your core message and your offer.

You will need to experiment and see what works best for your landing page. If you already have a landing page, what traffic sources have the best cost per acquisition? Can you scale these traffic sources up? Push your most profitable traffic sources to the limits. Once that traffic source is exhausted you can look for your next best option.

What traffic sources have the worst cost per acquisition? Often these are actually costing your business more than you expect. Eliminate these methods of traffic generation and remember to calculate your hours spent in the cost per acquisition.

What traffic sources are producing okay results? They might just need a little tinkering. Be creative. There could be a new angle or approach you could try. Keep playing with it to improve its performance or drop it if you feel you have exhausted its potential. It's about creating and refining a system to bring in a steady stream of new customers via your landing page.

Search Engine Optimisation and the Magic Bullet

"Hold on, I'll Google it…" Admit it, you Google! It's nothing to be ashamed of – everybody does it. That little phrase was unheard of not so long ago and today it echoes around offices, classrooms, and homes all over the world. It's testament to the way the Internet has established itself as an integral part of our daily lives.

There are billions of pages on the Internet and we need help navigating through them. If the Yellow Pages were billions of pages thick, you'd welcome a little help navigating that too. Enter search engines. A search engine is the Internet equivalent of the telephone's 'operator assistance' service. You tell them what you want and they find it for you. Would you devote your time and resources to building a website if nobody ever found it? Understanding search engines is critical if you want your website to be found online.

To perform well in search engines, you must think like a search engine. Search engines are basically huge databases with huge lists of websites. They try to list websites according to what they are about and list the most relevant websites for any given search, towards the top of the results. They are 'crawler' or 'spider-based' directories that 'crawl' the web according to a request and return relevant results. The key role of Search Engine Optimisation (SEO) is to ensure that your business is visible in the results when a relevant search is made. Simply put, SEO is the process of ensuring that your target audience can find you online through search engines.

If you already have a website, it does not necessarily mean it is recognised, or indexed by search engines. Likewise, because one of your web pages has found its way into the search engines, does not mean all your web pages have. For your pages to be indexed, they first need to be found by search engines, and then the content needs to be understood. If the search engines cannot understand what your webpage is about, then bad luck, they will not index you.

There is a lot of misinformation about SEO these days. There are many strategies and tips out there that are out-dated or confusing to most business owners. There are many SEO specialists claiming quick and effective results, often not telling you exactly what they're doing. Be careful selecting SEO providers like this. While they may produce short-term results, it could come back to bite you later! The Search Engines don't like people who try to game the system and if you keep some simple principles in mind you shouldn't have to.

Stick with these basic SEO principles and you can't go too far wrong:

- Provide high quality, unique content

- Structure your website so it is easy to navigate

- Use high quality, clean code so search engines can understand it

- Regularly update your website with fresh, up-to-date information

- Use words your target market may search for (keywords)

Most business people who have a website want more traffic. They want to sell more products or services, and gain more exposure. Understand it's not just about generating website traffic, but high quality traffic that is interested in what you do.

Consider your website virtual real estate. It's all about "Location, Location, Location". If bricks and mortar businesses can have prime locations, the same is true online. The first page of the search engine results is the "Main Street" of the online world. The web is a big place, and it's easy to get lost. Make sure your website can be seen and your voice heard above the clamour of businesses jostling for attention. An impressive website is useless in the absence of visitors. It's pointless creating a visually stunning website if few people ever see it. It's better to create a simple, yet effective presence.

When creating a website, it's not only human visitors you need to consider. You also need to make your website attractive to search engines to earn their respect. If you are competing for a keyword you believe to be profitable, your competitors are probably doing the same. While you might gain top ranking now, you could drop off quickly if you don't set up your SEO by following the basic SEO principles above.

Want the SEO Magic Bullet?

The SEO magic bullet is this: Fresh, original, relevant, high-quality content, written primarily for people and not search engines. That's part of the reason why there is an entire chapter dedicated to Content Marketing later in this book. Search engines focus on providing the best possible service for web-users conducting searches. If they lose sight of this goal, they will lose their users and in turn their business. The users are the "product" that their business model depends upon.

Give the search engines what they want – a fantastic website with fantastic content that they can see is relevant. By keeping this simple concept front of mind when working on SEO, you should future-proof your efforts, no matter what search engine algorithm changes are made. More about that later.

Keywords

Keywords are simply words or phrases people search for when using search engines like Google. What keywords would people needing your products or services search for, to find a business like yours? These keywords should be used throughout your website regularly, within great quality content. This will help your search engine ranking, based on these words or phrases.

The more unique your keyword, the easier it is to rank highly in search engines because fewer businesses are competing for it. It's also likely to be very specific to what your business does, so it's great to target. Be unique and be specific to simplify your SEO strategy.

Break your website into key areas you would like to target and be specific with your language. This way your keywords will naturally fit within specific pages. It helps to use keywords in your headings and page title. The goal is to select keywords with high search volumes and relatively low competition.

Think about your keywords from your customers' perspective and identify what terms they are likely to search for online. There are many programs you can purchase to help identify what keywords are likely to work best for you. The Google Keyword Planner is a great place to start. For my latest recommendations visit www.simplemanifesto.com/members

Poor Quality, Complex Coding

Poor quality coding may not only make your website display incorrectly on some browsers and devices, it also impacts SEO. Website programming standards and practices change over time, so it's important to review old websites according to current standards.

Some web developers offer a "Website Health Check" or a "Website Audit" that is worthwhile taking advantage of. You will find the latest tools and resources to assess your website coding in our 'Members Only' resources at www.simplemanifesto.com/members

Each piece of the web development puzzle has an impact on your SEO. Some things help and some hinder your results. Many web developers invest all their time and resources into the look and feel of the website. While that may be helpful, it can be counter-productive if you overdo it.

Web developers may try to use all of the latest fads, ignoring the fact that search engines may overlook them, making the websites unfriendly to the search engines.

Don't create complicated "User Experiences" requiring complex coding. Your website is not the place for your web developer to showcase all of his or her skills. Using complex 'tricks' can slow your website down, make it difficult to use, and perform poorly in search engines. Simplify!

Images

Optimising images for search engines is not something that all webmasters do. The common practise is to add the image to the content without any regard to its title, size, or tags. Convenient as that may be, it's not recommended. Here's how you can optimise your images in three simple steps.

1. Optimise your images size

Large image files slow down your website's loading speed. Find a compromise between size and quality. Choose the smallest file size possible that doesn't affect the quality of how the image looks. If you want to post a photo of a product for example, don't choose the maximum quality Jpeg file when high quality looks just as good and is a much smaller file size.

2. Add keywords to your image file name

Images with filenames containing keywords tend to help your rankings in search engines. It should be relevant to the actual image itself. We never condone trying to trick search engines. As mentioned, this can come back to bite you.

3. Add Alt-text

Search engines use the alt-text to figure out what an image is about. Without alt-text, it's difficult for search engines to 'understand' and classify your images.

Don't get overwhelmed with all of this technical stuff. Your web developers should be taking care of this for you but many won't unless you ask, so include something like this in your brief to them:

"Please ensure all images are optimised in size without losing too much visual quality, named using keywords where it's appropriate, and have alt-text using keywords that also describe the images well."

How the SEO Rules Have Changed

Unfortunately, the SEO world is full of shady characters, dodgy practices and misinformation. You would be better off doing no SEO at all than to get involved with 'black-hat' SEO. Black-hat SEO is about trying to trick search engines to rank a website more highly than it deserves. These strategies could destroy your business online. While they often generate more traffic to a website initially, sooner or later the search engines find out and down-grade or completely black-list the website. If they get the impression you are trying to cheat your way to the top, get ready for a world of pain.

'White-hat' SEO strategies are ethical, high quality techniques designed to earn the respect, and traffic, from the search engines. They are the only strategies I recommend and endorse.

Search engines change algorithms to provide a better service to people using their search features by removing the 'bad eggs'. If you are an ethical, white-hat marketer these algorithm updates are often good news for you. When an algorithm change is introduced, your competitors who use black-hat SEO drop away in the search results and you naturally move up the results page. If, on the other hand, you've been adversely affected by an algorithm change, it will likely sound the alarm bells, making you understand that the tactics you are using are not beneficial long term.

Over the years, Google have introduced algorithm changes that have largely put an end to black-hat SEO techniques, which exploited backlinks, over-optimisation, and keyword stuffing to improve the ranking of websites. Quality has beaten quantity, and websites that featured a large quantity of poor quality backlinks, keyword-stuffed articles, or duplicate content were heavily penalised. We will explore some of these techniques later so you know what to avoid. You can also Google the topics to find out more about them if you are interested. Just don't get sucked into any tricky strategy.

I know all this jargon can get confusing and you may delegate your SEO work in good faith to specialists. I encourage outsourcing to local professionals, however when it comes to SEO, it's important you understand the dangers of blindly trusting someone to do the right thing by you.

Black-hat SEO techniques change over time as programmers try to beat the system in order to rank higher, while the Search Engines develop new technology to stop the cheats. If you think your developer can consistently beat the collective knowledge of the search engine programmers, good luck to you! If you have invested in SEO now or even years ago, and you are not sure what your SEO provider did for you, you could be sitting in a dangerous position right now.

If your SEO provider is promising results quickly but does not tell you how, you should be sceptical. It's likely they will be using black-hat techniques. Once the search engines find out how your website is manipulating the system, you could find your website punished as a result. It is not worth the risk.

There are many businesses who simply don't understand the reason behind their sudden loss of traffic and one of their most valuable online assets, their website ranking. They sack the SEO provider but the SEO guy walks away with whatever they were paid up until that point, and you are left behind with a damaged website that can be very difficult to rectify. Take advantage of trustworthy, expert knowledge and experience, and ignore the fads.

Google's business model hinges on their ability to help people find the best sources of information when a search is done. Their algorithms are always being improved and are becoming more sophisticated so they can continue to provide a fantastic user experience. That's why they are so successful, and that's why they guard against manipulative SEO techniques. Fair enough, I'd say.

It's easy to work out if a particular search engine optimisation strategy is white-hat or black-hat. If the strategy involves providing a great website with excellent, useful content, then it is white-hat. If it is trying to trick search engines, then it is black-hat.

Backlinks

Backlinks, or inbound links to your website from other, well respected websites that are relevant to what you do, can increase your traffic. For this reason, people often try to build up their inbound links with a variety of dodgy tactics. In years gone by there were reciprocal link directories. This is where webmasters connected to swap links with each other. We have also seen article syndication and article spinning. If you don't know what that is, it's probably best you don't! These old SEO tactics eventually lose their effectiveness and, in fact, have a negative impact on SEO now. There will always be scams and tricks available to manipulate search engines. Avoid them!

Think about SEO realistically, and always consider the long-term effects of your efforts. When you do SEO, long-lasting results will take time to develop. Use SEO tactics that are legitimate and are even recommended by search engines themselves. The goal of your SEO is to be recognised as the authority in your industry, and gain links from other websites based on your website's merit. If your website is authoritative and commands the respect of others in your field, then it will become one that people will want to visit and link to. This is the ideal way of gaining great backlinks and, in turn, high search results.

The general rule of thumb is to avoid backlinks that:

- Come from 'dodgy neighbourhoods' such as adult websites.

- Use the same keyword-rich anchor text for many backlinks.

- Use site-wide footer links.

- Come from 'spammy' websites built for the sole purpose of creating backlinks.

- Come from websites that are not related in any way to yours.

- Come from web pages with lots of external links.

If you have backlinks like this now, get rid of them. You could try to clean up your backlink damage yourself, but it can be incredibly time consuming and sometimes it can be difficult to undo the damage when you have been slapped by the search engines. Go back and remove any black-hat strategies you have used, clean up your website, and implement stringent quality control to earn their trust back. Good luck with that. It might take some time. SAs should consider outsourcing the clean up. Leave it to the specialists and focus your energies on the more positive aspects of your new SEO strategy.

Keywords Density

Keyword density is the percentage that a particular keyword is used on a web page in comparison to all the other text on the page. Over the years, much has been said about keyword density, there are even tools online to measure it, and many people have different opinions on what percentages are good. Forget about percentages. If the content is useful and reads well, it is optimised well. If customers respond to it, it works. If you focus on a specific niche within your business on each webpage, you will end up with great content that search engines love and your visitors are actually interested in. Once you have these essentials in place you could look at introducing keywords to give your website a small boost. You will probably find you have some keywords naturally in your content anyway. There are many tools that will help suggest different keywords to use, but you should get the basics right first.

Make sure the URL is relevant for the page

Use Search Engine Friendly URL's. This means using something like this: www.yourwebsite.com/article-name as opposed to: www.yourwebsite.com/gen.pl?id=basic23.php. It's much tidier and is more user-friendly for humans and search engines. Most website software these days will let you edit the URL, so if you don't like the auto-generated one, you can change it to something you like. Normally it's best that the URL is the same as the heading, however if the heading is long, you can shorten the URL. This is great if you want to make your URL more memorable to promote in print-based marketing. Use keywords where it makes sense to do so, but only if it's relevant to the content on the page.

Write a good meta-description

It's well worth the effort to write a unique meta-description for each web page. It's the piece of text that often shows up in the search results under the link. Think of it like a mini-ad for your web page. Firstly, write something enticing so people will click the link. Secondly, you should consider the keywords you want to rank well for, and use them. Remember, you must always consider humans first, and search engines second.

Test your programming

There are tools online to test how friendly your website is to search engines. Visit www.simplemanifeso.com/members for my current recommendations. Chances are, many of the findings will not make much sense if you are not a web developer. Send them to your web developer for their input. As an SA, the purpose is not to do all the work yourself, but to find out what needs to be done and outsource it to experts in the field.

Duplicate Content

If you are posting content that is not seen as original, this can cause problems in search engines. Even if you have permission to republish the content and don't run fowl of plagiarism laws, you are likely to have SEO problems. You don't want duplicate content that is elsewhere online because the search engines will only give credit to one source. If you are hiring a writer, ensure they work to high ethical standards and don't plagiarise work. They should also understand SEO, so they not only avoid duplicate content, but produce the best possible traffic through the content they write.

"Things in excess become their opposite."
– Timothy Ferris

SEO Overkill

This may sound counter-intuitive, so stick with me. Too much SEO is as bad for your business as too little SEO, if not worse. One way SEO can kill your website is through keywords.

If you stuff your pages with keywords hoping to improve your SEO, you could be doing more harm than good. This can also happen if you choose to target too few keywords. The temptation will be to jam them in everywhere you can. It's better to create a broad range of keywords and use them where it makes sense to do so. Leave them out if it's going to read poorly. Keywords should be sprinkled throughout your content, as they naturally occur, particularly in headings.

If you are too restrictive with your keywords and what you write about, you'll end up writing terrible content. Writing for search engines only, is a sure-fire way of lowering the quality of your content. This is particularly relevant when blogging, which we will explore in the following chapters.

The best writing often occurs spontaneously. By restricting your keywords and topics too narrowly, you take away the creativity and fun of writing. Many bloggers would stand a better chance of getting good rankings and traffic if they simply forgot about SEO, and focussed their efforts on creating something that is interesting, engaging, and sharable.

When you exaggerate the importance of SEO, you end up unconsciously writing content for search engines and not for people. The quality of the content might be okay and optimised, however you will be tempted to waffle and pad it out just for the sake of writing more words. SEO is great, until it starts affecting the quality of your website.

Focus on connecting with people, and not on perfecting SEO. Do the right thing by your human readers, and the SEO will take care of itself in many ways.

The missing SEO ingredient

Having high quality coding and content are the two biggest keys to SEO, but that doesn't mean you should ignore the aesthetics. This is one of the most overlooked aspects of SEO. Making your website more attractive can increase your traffic and improve your conversion rates. Search engines are getting smarter all the time. They know if visitors don't spend long on your website and presume it's a poor website.

Often visitors don't stay on a website because it looks terrible. If you want more traffic, make your website more attractive. When it comes to SEO, think about the complete package including content, coding, and the visual message. When your website looks great to humans, there's a good chance search engines will notice and rank you highly.

Don't ever become too dependent on search engines. If SEO is the only marketing strategy you are implementing, and you are depending on it to provide a source of income, you are in a dangerous position. Website traffic is a fantastic way to build up your customer base, however you should never have all your eggs in one basket, particularly one you have little control over. You never want to have your livelihood at the mercy of search engines.

Spread your marketing investment of time and money across a few areas, so if one ever fails you have others that will keep your business running. All your free traffic doesn't need to come from search engines either. Other sources of free traffic include:

- Newsletter subscriptions

- Sharing links via social media

- JV's (joint ventures) with other businesses so you can market to their databases

- The list goes on so let's leave that for the next Lens...

position

Noun:

The state of being placed where one has an advantage over one's rivals or competitors.

Synonyms:

Advantage, the upper hand, the edge, the whip hand, primacy, the catbird seat, the box seat

(in team games) a role assigned to a particular player based on the location in which they play.

(Credit Google.com - edited)

Positioning is a bit of a buzz-word in marketing these days. However, there still seems to be a lot of confusion about how to apply it in business. Let's simplify it! This lens is about taking what we established in the previous lenses and using it to establish a rock solid position in the marketplace. Positioning is not another marketing principle you need to work on. It's a bit like branding: Simple if you get your foundations right and don't let the gurus complicate it for you.

As soon as people come into contact with your business, they start to categorise it. This happens if they contact you through an advertising campaign or a face-to-face meeting. They need to understand who you are, what you do, and why that's important, and for you to be successful they have to be able to do this quickly and easily. This is why the SA is always reinforcing their position in the marketplace.

Content Marketing for Mortals and Machines

Your message is what positions you, and there is no greater way to share that message than through Content Marketing. Content Marketing has become increasingly popular, especially for thought leaders who use it to connect with their customers and subtly market their products or services. When it comes to text, online content can be a little different to writing for print-based media. People tend to scan through website content quickly, not reading word-for-word, so headings, sub-headings, and bullet points are more important. That's what is most likely to be read, and it's also the content search engines pay the most attention to.

It's no accident the word "Authority" has the word "Author" in it. Content positions you as the expert in your chosen industry, and helps increase your website traffic. You don't even need to produce the content yourself, your priority is to drive the thinking behind it.

Content is king online, yet many businesses struggle to create content that produces results. Part of the problem is the way we often define content. When most of us think content, we think text. While text is important, there are many other forms of content to consider.

When you think content, think about videos, podcasts, photography, diagrams, and graphics. Content is anything a business produces to communicate a message. Each form of content has its own advantages and disadvantages and suits different purposes.

Humans First, Search Engines Second

I've said it before, and I'll say it again – always think like your target-market first, not a search engine. The search engines are becoming more and more advanced and their goal is to provide the best possible websites for the keywords people are searching for. This should also be your goal. Align your intentions with that of the search engines and you can't go too far wrong.

If your content is attractive to your readers, then chances are, it will be attractive to the search engines too. Think of your content as a step in your sales funnel. You will have many visitors and a percentage of these will convert into sales. It's about getting as many potential customers to visit your website as you can, and finding a way to keep them coming back for more.

While content may seem free if you create it yourself, it costs time and energy to produce. Place a high value on your time and energy when running your business, because it's limited and may be better spent elsewhere. If you don't enjoy writing, then don't. You can outsource the writing to a professional or ignore having a content strategy completely. More on that later.

We believe that the best Web content optimization strategy is something as old as journalism itself: the shocking truth and the authentic opinion.

– Nick Denton

Blogging

Update your website as often as you can with content that appeals to your target market. One of the easiest ways to do this is to add a blog or articles section where you can add new content on a weekly basis. As mentioned in the previous lens, high quality content is one of the most important aspects of SEO, so this will move you up the search results. Creating a content strategy based around blogging is the perfect way to get started.

While writing content for your blog may come easy for some, maintaining it while juggling your other activities may not be so simple. If you want to be a successful blogger, consistently post interesting content. Yes, it takes time, and yes, there are always other tasks needing your attention. Just remember you don't need to do it all yourself.

For most of us, our blog is not our business, it's simply a marketing tool to engage our audience. It can be fun, and a chance to let the creative juices flow. It can help you share ideas and become a perceived leader in your industry, but it does take planning. Create a schedule and allocate time, or money for outsourcing if you choose to do so.

Decide on your content style and tone. Get this right and you'll grow your readership over time. Encourage your readers to come back for more. Often it is better to write all the content you need for a month in one sitting, so you can set aside the time and focus on your writing. Blogs tend to be less formal than other content in your website, but you need to select a tone and style that you are comfortable with. Humour may be appropriate for some markets and not others. It comes down to your standpoint as a business and an individual, as well as who your customers are. The SA knows that it's about personality and human interaction. While your blog should focus on providing information that has relevance to your target market, it's also an opportunity to highlight who you are. Use illustrations and examples from your own personal life. Your customers will be buying into you, the person, not just your products or services.

Write about the common challenges and problems your customers are facing, and offer viable solutions. Show your readers you empathise with them, and you understand their problems. There can sometimes be a fear that you will provide your most valuable content freely and have nothing more to give. I have found this is a common fear that is rarely true. The more you give and the more creative thoughts you have flowing, the more you grow and increase the value you can provide others. The bottom-line is, if you have interesting content in your blog you will draw in many more potential clients who make the giving worth the investment.

> *"The problem with the Internet is that it gives you everything - reliable material and crazy material. So the problem becomes, how do you discriminate?"*
> **– Umberto Eco**

When a potential customer reads a blog, it's usually because it answers a need or question they have. People don't usually look for blogs to provide a direct sales pitch so a subtle approach is more effective. There's no harm in the occasional plug, as long as you keep the focus on providing useful information.

People often ask what the right length of content is. The simple answer is, as long as it needs to be to get your message across and no longer. If that means writing 300 words, great; but sometimes it may take many more words than that.

Here are some thoughts to inspire you and get the creative juices flowing:

- Publish content that you could sell. Insider's tips and professional advice is the best. Don't be afraid! Some will take your content and shop elsewhere, but others will read it and feel reassurance that you're the expert they need.

- Interview awesome people from your niche. Tailor the interview in a way to get as many tips and advice from the interviewee as possible.

- Be sincere. Talk about your failures as openly as you talk about your successes. Don't be afraid to be personal.

- Draw inspiration from newspapers and magazines. Look for the sensational, for the intriguing, for the provocative. It's a goldmine for great headlines.

Polarising Headlines

Make your headlines polarising. Some will love it and others may hate it. We've already established this is a good thing. You will get attention and it's far better to have a few buy-in than to politely appease the masses that will never commit.

The few that do buy-in will be far more likely to become raving fans and advocates of your business who tell others about your business and values. Guess what? These people who buy-in hang out with other people just like them, people who share their values, values that are congruent with yours. They share your passion with others who share your passion and word-of-mouth marketing gains effortless momentum. Now that's simple marketing!

Marketers often have processes they follow in writing articles, especially if they are designed to boost website traffic. Most start off by doing some keyword research. Next, they will probably start with the body of the article, by trying to include keywords. Once they are complete, they will probably try to come up with a catchy headline.

Flip this process on its head and come up with the headline first. Your headline is what will attract clicks and it is a vital part of any article. Of course, the body of the article needs to be high quality and support the headline.

Never sacrifice the quality of your headline for keywords. It's awesome if you can get a keyword in your headline, but it's not always achievable. Run over your article when you are proof reading it and give yourself a little keyword boost here and there where you can without damaging how it reads.

- **Headlines that ask questions** catch people's attention quickly. Highlight a common need your target market experiences and allude to the fact that you have the solution.

- **Lists tend to do well,** particularly when they are an odd number. For example '7 Ways to A B C." or "9 Laws to X Y Z."

- **'How to' headlines are a great idea** when you are struggling for a headline. Often people search online to find out how to do something. They are looking for instructions and guidelines. They want to find an expert like you. The options are endless.

- **Make your target audience feel special** by using "you" or "your" in the article's headline. This will make them feel that you are talking to them directly. It will make them feel that you are specifically addressing their situation.

- **Humour or controversy can go a long way** in attracting readers. People cannot resist a good laugh or controversial topic. People love anything that inspires debate, and it's bound to get a response.

Website users want the information they need pronto! The headline is simply there to grab attention and get people to read the rest of the content. Most people won't read past the first two paragraphs. Your website's headlines and first paragraphs must answer the single most important question: What's in it for me?

"One should use common words to say uncommon things"

– Arthur Schopenhauer

There are many business owners

who know their industry so well, they forget to explain things in simple terms. People are time poor and tend to rush through content online trying to find the information they need quickly. They know there are many other websites they could look at to get what they need fast.

Choose a title that's search-engine friendly

Your page title is different to the heading. The title of a post can appear at the top of the browser window and is used by search engines when they provide search results. It can be the same as the heading of the post itself, or it may be different since its purpose is slightly different. Website software is often set to automatically make the title the same as the headline. This is convenient, but not always to your advantage for two reasons:

1. The length of your headline may not be appropriate for the search engine results.

2. You may want to use keywords in the title that are not in the headline but are still relevant for the content.

Video Content

The popularity of online video marketing has increased rapidly over the past few years. People have become increasingly visual and are now using the Internet even more than they watch television. The capabilities of the Internet have also increased rapidly. Where once it was impossible for most people to view a video online, now almost everyone in the Western world has fast enough Internet connections to handle it. In fact, many people now watch full-length movies on home PC's or Smart TV's. When video is used well, it has the power to reach huge numbers of people at no additional cost to you. Many web users prefer video over written content, so you are likely to keep visitors on your website longer if you include video. The search engines like websites where visitors stick around so embedding great videos will help your SEO efforts.

Video can break barriers between your business and your target market, creating the rapport you need. Ideally the viewer will begin to know, like and trust you. The problem is, many marketers find getting started with video content daunting.

You don't need to spend a fortune on video marketing. In fact, in some cases you could possibly do it with the tools you already have at your disposal, or with a few low or no cost tools you can download

"Do not let your grand ambitions stand in the way of small but meaningful accomplishments."

– Bryant McGill

online. Of course you could use a professional production company, if a high-end premium quality video is a better fit for your purpose. It will probably look more professional but it doesn't always produce better results. Remember what I said about stock photos, be careful not to look too cheesy or be misaligned with your target market. Your videos should remain congruent with who you are and the intended purpose of the video. After all, it's about the content, not the production. In some cases, DIY videos are more successful due to their authentic feel. It feels like you are engaging with a real person, not a slick hired gun, or an actor. Your unique standpoint should help you decide if it's best to hire professionals or do it yourself.

The success of online video is not determined by the size of your budget or the amount of time you are prepared to invest. To maximise your results consider the following:

- Your video should have a clear structure and a purpose

- It should identify a problem your target market has

- Present a solution to this problem

- It should direct your target audience to take the next step

It's the content and engaging nature of video that makes it work. What matters most is the ability to deliver a message clearly and effectively through the video. If you are going to DIY your videos and are prepared to spend a little, consider a digital camera with microphone input, microphone, and lighting equipment. Create a simple system for yourself and focus most of your energy on making your video informative, useful, and entertaining; not on the technical production.

While you could self-host videos or use a professional grade, video hosting system, YouTube is usually fine and can be embedded into your website. Even if you do choose to host your videos elsewhere, it's still worthwhile adding it to YouTube if it's marketing-based material. YouTube has a massive amount of traffic and therefore has a huge capacity to direct traffic your way, particularly if you know how to leverage it.

Submit your videos everywhere you can. The hard work is already done creating the video, so make the most of it and submit it to a variety of video directories. Embed it in your blog and post it in social media. The idea is to get as many people as possible to see it, and hopefully share it with others.

Write a great headline and include a call-to-action and backlink in the description when you post your video to YouTube. Verbally tell your viewers what to do next. If they don't take action and do what you request, chances are they will keep viewing other videos, possibly your competitors. You could also show your website address across the bottom of the video if visiting your website is the call-to-action.

Content for the Time Poor

Re-work, Re-create, Re-purpose, Re-imagine

Most businesses produce potential marketing content without even knowing it. Think about the emails and proposals written, the phone calls made, the PowerPoint presentations created. It's all content. The problem is it is often presented one-to-one. It's created once, to be presented to one recipient. What if you could somehow capture this content and re-purpose it for content marketing? What if you could transform your content so it can be viewed by many? It might need a little tweaking to suit the new purpose, but the bulk of the hard work is already done. Here's a common re-purposing structure you could adapt and experiment with:

"Simplicity is ultimately a matter of focus."
– Ann Voskamp

- Workshop delivered and recorded to Video

- Video transcribed and edited to become an e-Book

- e-Book broken down into articles/ blogs by adding introductions and conclusions

- Blog posts promoted through social media

There are various forms of this kind of model. Some use podcasts rather than workshops for example. Some rework a few e-Books into a printed, physical book. This way, all the different ways content is delivered serves different purposes:

- Workshop to engage interested people live (free or paid)

- Video to get people to the workshops, make an enquiry or visit your website

- e-Book as bait to build your database

- Blog to get the attention of search engines and most importantly, humans.

It's the same content in a variety of formats so a larger number of people can consume it. Let your target market consume your content, however they choose to. Just don't re-purpose or re-use the same text on different websites or webpages. That will be seen as duplicate content and, as previously highlighted, this can cause issues.

Re-purposed content can be produced by a Virtual Assistant who can do the heavy lifting for you. Virtual Assistants are like Personal Assistants who work from home and usually communicate with you over the internet. We will look at outsourcing to Virtual Assistants and other professionals later, so stay tuned.

It's often helpful to think more like a publisher than a sales person when it comes to producing content. Sales letters and the like have their place, but that isn't the kind of content I am suggesting here. I'm talking about taking your raw content and adapting it so it's engaging and interesting. Publishers consider the seasonal timing, current events, and news to engage their audience. Often marketers miss these opportunities. If you can create interaction with your content, for example, you might provide comments on your blog, you will benefit from the user generated content. Now that's a simple content strategy.

Tell the story and build upon it. Co-creating the story with people involved along the way is a great way to add depth to your content. For example, if you were to take content from a proposal and adjust it into a case study you could ask for feedback or a testimonial from the customer to feature in your new piece, giving it more life.

Have you previously produced hard-copy newsletters, articles, or flyers? You can save yourself time and effort by re-purposing this material. It may even kick-start ideas that take you on a completely new tangent. Starting with something to work from, typically takes less effort than sitting in front of a blank screen and hoping for inspiration. The opportunities are endless.

A word of caution. Avoid churning out rubbish just to make use of all your content. Ask yourself the following:

- Will it engage my target market?

- What impression will it create?

- Will people share it?

- What are the possible positive outcomes?

- Are there any possible negative outcomes?

How to Hijack the News

Businesses can use hot news topics to get more attention, more traffic, more backlinks, more followers and, as a result, more customers. Social media is the place to be if you want to pick up these hot topics early so you can be one of the first commenting on the topic. Let's face it, nobody wants to read the same news twice, so be one of the first or have a unique twist to the story. We will explore social media in the following chapters.

Here's how to hijack the hottest news for your content marketing:

1. Stay updated with the latest news in your niche by following other thought leaders in your industry. Only follow the best, so you can quickly sift through the information.

2. Hand-pick the pieces of news that will have the biggest impact on your target audience.

3. Interpret the news. Don't rehash someone else's opinion, tailor your message to your market. What does the story mean for your niche? How will it impact your readers? What will change? To engage your readers, interpret the news from their perspective, to show what it means to them.

4. Don't be afraid to be controversial. You could write an opposing view to what others are saying. Taking a nonconformist standpoint is often what brings you the most interaction.

Be aware of what's happening around

"There is nothing so stable as change."

– Bob Dylan

you, in the news and topics of interest for the people you associate with. Follow the trends and keep an eye on what complementary businesses and competitors are saying online. There are often opportunities you can take advantage of, if you know what is happening around you. You may come across complaints about your industry or your competitors. Listen to what they are saying and consider how you can respond.

Re-ignite your Passion

I have another confession to make! I love writing but, from time to time, I struggle to come up with something that is fresh and exciting for my readers. Sometimes I can sit in front of the computer screen for hours without getting anything useful written. If you are a writer or are creative, you've probably experienced something similar at one point or another. After a while, your content can seem a little lacklustre.

Are your readers still engaged with what you have to say?

What can you do to recharge and refresh your content?

Maybe you are having trouble finding fresh topics to write on. Maybe you are struggling to come up with something useful and relevant for your target audience. You may be feeling that you're losing the attention of your readers. Don't lose heart, we all feel like this at times and need to re-ignite our passion.

Based on what I've experienced myself and what I've discussed with a number of people, there are simple ways to help alleviate the pressure and get back on track. It can be slightly different for each individual, however this advice helps many people I speak with.

Find a new way to write. Draw inspiration from current events, and use stories in industry publications or newsletters as a springboard. Customers will respond to concise and interesting information, that either helps them with an issue, or tells them something they find interesting.

We can get stale if we approach life the same way each and every day.

It could be as simple as handwriting your new content on a notepad first or taking your laptop to the park and writing something new. Changing your environment can change the way you view the world and the way you write. Do something to break the monotony. Coming up with a topic can be hard sometimes. It can help to formulate a series ahead of time so you can get into the swing of writing quickly and easily.

"No matter what people tell you, words and ideas can change the world."
– Robin Williams

There is a multitude of content online and offline. Try something you haven't looked at before. You could listen to podcasts or watch some videos online. You could read an interesting book. You could also think a little laterally and use stories you observe in your day-to-day life to get a fresh message across. If you are into movies, they are a great source of inspiration for many content producers.

Take advantage of any travel time and load some interesting podcasts to your phone or MP3 player. It doesn't need to be about the topic you cover in your content, anything you find interesting could inspire a different approach. I enjoy watching TED talks at random, it is a way I open myself to new thoughts and ideas.

The Social Media Revolution

The social media world is still relatively new and is changing rapidly, so to publish the specifics on how to use a certain platform in this book is not viable. However, the overriding principles shouldn't change and that's what we will be focussing on in this chapter. For more specific, up-to-date tools and tips visit www.simplemanifesto.com/members

Trust me, I've tried everything on social media to find out what works. Repeat: Everything! This book means you don't have to go through this painful process of trial and error. You probably want to use social media as there is a lot of buzz around its marketing capabilities these days. Let's make one thing perfectly clear: Social media isn't for everyone – at least not in the way most of the so-called experts suggest you use it.

With its minimal financial costs and potentially deep penetration into the market, social media marketing represents a great opportunity for many businesses. However, you need to consider the time it will cost you. Remember you must place a high value on your time. Think about your long-term vision: Does social media enhance or distract you from your objectives.

There are two schools of thought to consider when it comes to social media. The first is to form meaningful conversations, positioning your business as the experts in your niche. This keeps the 'social' in your social media strategy. The other option is to use it as a broadcasting tool for your message, with links to your website content or offers. Many will frown upon this second option. But it saves bucket loads of time and maximises your results. Also, there are tools to help you automate and schedule your social media activity. For my latest recommendations visit www.simplemanifesto.com/members

The general population are becoming savvy social beasts online and when it comes to activity, social networking sites like Facebook, Google+, Twitter, and LinkedIn are being used more than search engines. It's a mindless addiction sometimes similar to that faced by Jack, the Ice addict we learnt from in Lens 1. It can be like a nervous twitch for some, and a compulsive addiction for many. Don't fall into the trap. Remember that being an SA is about avoiding busy-ness and focusing on effectiveness.

Before you do anything else with social media, you should first get your website pumping. Your website should be the mothership of your online marketing. It should be integrated with social media so visitors can like, tweet, and share your web pages or blog posts. It's far better they do the sharing for you, rather than you sitting there doing all the heavy lifting. With social media, you can let others use their relationships to build your business. That's the easy part. Next, setup your own social media accounts and add links to your website since that will be your mother-ship online.

Your prospects want to connect with interesting people, so don't be boring in social media. It's great to get noticed frequently, but if you want to engage your prospects, show your personality and be memorable. Read through what you have written and get rid of the boring bits before submitting. Focus on being someone that people identify with, that way customers identify with your business.

Think about the photo you use in your profiles. It is the first thing visitors see and, if you're honest, the first thing you look at when you visit someone else's profile. Your picture should present you in the best possible light. Express your personality in the style of photo you use. For example, if you are a fun, adventurous person, show it. It's usually a bad idea to use a logo rather than a photograph in your profile picture. Social media is about personal interactions so a friendly human face is more effective.

Consider the intentions of social networking sites, however you don't need to play by someone else's rules. It's true, people don't want to be "sold to". Then again, social media is filled with people who need the products and services you could be offering. Some people may be irritated by your spruiking, but guess what, they probably were never going to be your customer anyway. People who actually benefit from your product or service will likely be thankful they saw what you posted. However, be careful to

"99.5 percent of the people that walk around and say they are a social media expert or guru are clowns. We are going to live through a devastating social media bubble."

– Gary Vaynerchuk

avoid harassing your friends and followers; get the balance right.

People want to create meaningful connections and conversations using social media, so don't go looking for a quick sale. Don't be that annoying Multi-Level Marketing (MLM) person always trying to recruit people or sell something you don't need. There's no need to burn your friends like that.

Social media is a place to attract attention, not to blatantly advertise your business every opportunity you get. Abusing this principle will ensure your social media is a complete waste of time. Most users don't log into social media with commercial intent, but to interact with friends, meet new people, or waste time in their 9 to 5 job. If it happens that a good offer comes their way they may take it, especially if it's shared by a friend. Don't expect users to be actively looking for special deals or offers, because they won't. If they wanted to do that, they would use a search engine.

Social media has the great advantage of providing not only instant exposure, but also feedback. Feedback is crucial for any business. Positive feedback fills you and your team with confidence, while negative feedback highlights how you can improve.

The Branding Myth

We have covered many of the branding lies many of the so-called guru's spruik in previous Lenses. Here's a big one. Many will tell you to use social media just to increase brand awareness. It's a terrible goal. Social media is great to create awareness, however the end goal for any business should be more than that. Don't buy into the fluffy, feel-good ideas some Muppet will try to sell you. A lot of junk gets passed off as branding and social media often gets shoved into this fuzzy label.

Look at verifiable, traceable results that you can measure and validate. The "brand" exposure will happen naturally as part of the process but it's not the end goal. Big business that throw large sums of cash around can use social media for branding. They have the financial muscle to make this kind of strategy work. One of the biggest reasons they use it is for damage control. Hopefully you don't have too many spot-fires on social media that you need to deal with like large corporations sometimes do.

Busy-ness: Counting the Costs

All of us can rattle off a list of friends and family who seem addicted to using social media. Some business people rationalise it by calling it a 'marketing tool'. If it truly is marketing, then show me the results. Count the cost and measure its usefulness in your business. How many hours do you put in, and what kind of return are you getting? Many people use 'social media marketing' as a guise to what it really is, procrastination.

The worst addicts are those who use a variety of social media platforms jumping from one place to the next all day. What a distraction. They have allowed their social media to take over their whole working day. For these people, saying they are going to jump onto social media for a minute is as realistic as an alcoholic saying they will only have one drink. It's not going to happen!

Social media can be a massive distraction and time-waster, especially if you follow some of the so-called experts. An SA knows that success is about minimising distractions. If email or social media consumes much of your working day consider working for the first couple of hours a day focused on your big goals before the distractions set in, or schedule set times for these activities.

"People who avoid the brick walls - all power to ya, but we all have to hit them sometimes in order to push through to the next level, to evolve."

– Jennifer Aniston

Most people I meet believe social media can be powerful for business. They understand it can help them reach new audiences and acquire new customers, however they wrongly assume it's free. Social media marketing is not free. Unlike paid advertising, social media marketing doesn't have to cost money (although you can pay for increased exposure). You can create social media accounts for free and start sharing for free. That said, social media marketing needs to be maintained to be effective, and that maintenance requires time.

The deeper you plunge into social media, the more time it will kill. The more time it kills, the less time you will have for more important tasks. You might get some misguided sense of satisfaction from that busy feeling but it's not usually the best use of your time.

If you are using social media as a genuine marketing strategy, minimise your time spent to stay involved, while maximising its effect. Cut the fluff. Only read what is beneficial and productive to your business or you could find yourself stuck in cyberspace for hours each day.

It became popular a few years back to refer to the Internet as 'The information super highway'. Guess what, there are thousands of rubbish trucks on that highway, filled with junk, ready to dump right in your lap if you let them. Don't get sucked into a vortex of meaningless conversations.

It's not hard to use social media, but it does require work and persistence. Here are some tips:

- Decide what you hope to achieve through your social media marketing. For example, you may be promoting a product or service, using it for research, or testing marketing messages.

- Understand your followers. Think about why they would follow you, what they like, dislike, and above all, what they want. You will need to test your assumptions and develop your ideas as you make progress.

- What have you got to say? Consistently providing interesting information will keep your followers coming back for more. If you have a blog or articles as described in previous chapters, you will constantly have something fresh to share. Simply post the headline, description (if it fits), and link to the article. Job done!

We will discuss collaboration in a later chapter. Social media marketing is one area you should consider outsourcing if you do it at all. You provide the direction for the content and style and let someone else do the grunt work.

Many small business owners tend to undervalue their time and then wonder why they are working 15 hour days with little to show for it. Trust me, I've been there too and I've found the solution is to count the cost of your time.

Will social media work for you? Despite the ever-growing popularity of social media, not many businesses experience additional sales that can be easily correlated to their social media activity. When increases in sales do appear it's usually hard to assess the results, and the amount of time invested into social media, to decide whether all that effort was worth it. Having said that, it's something you may need to experiment with yourself. One thing I've noticed in my time is that social media seems to work better for B2C (Business to Consumer) companies than B2B (Business to Business). Why? There seems to be some common reasons: The purchase cycle in B2B tends to be longer, and customers buy products 'more rationally'. With B2C, purchases are done more impulsively and emotionally. B2C products are often about lifestyle and can seem more exciting, whereas B2B can often be a little boring.

Consider your product and service and whether it's something people will want to chat about online. Are you delivering something they want to share? If you are selling Haemorrhoid cream, it's probably not ideal for you. If you are a funeral home, I'm pretty sure you are not going to have a massive following of people wanting to hear about the latest deaths in your suburb. Most businesses are not as clear-cut as this. Take some educated guesses, test your assumptions, and experiment – it's all part of the process. Stay flexible so you can adapt and improve as you go.

If you are selling a product or service that is an area of passion or interest for people, social media can work well for you. For example, a boutique coffee shop recently started on social media and within a few days had a huge list of followers without any promotional effort. That's passion for you, and that's exactly what you need if you want your social media to be a success.

If you do bite the bullet and choose to use social media, you've got to use it. Similar to buying exercise equipment, owning it will not make you fit. It takes using the equipment correctly to make the biggest difference. There is no doubt that the proper use of social media networks can often help. It's like the 'miracle' exercise equipment many of us now have under the bed, or those who join gyms, we go crazy for a week or so attending every day, but eventually don't turn up at all. Some business owners go overboard early without the ability to maintain the activity. It is best to streamline your systems from the start and create an easy-to-follow schedule that you can maintain.

Social media can help you reach potential customers fast, but it also means your competitors can easily watch you too. Many of your new found "friends" are not prospects at all, they are your competitors, keeping an eye on you in the hope that they can rip off your next killer idea. Don't be deceived by the number of followers you have. There is one analytics tool that matters and it's not how many followers you have. It's the numbers that show up in your bank account.

If you are already involved in social media ask yourself this tough question: "How many customers have I gained through social media?" Be brutally honest with yourself.

New Breed PR

While advertising is what you say about yourself, PR (public relations) is what you encourage others to say about you or your business. It's the perception you create and encourage to be spread. It's about the position you create for your business. Gone are the days of the slimy PR specialist selling you the "promise" that he or she has contacts in powerful places. Content marketing enhanced by social media enables you to create your own PR.

Once upon a time, big business was able to influence traditional media outlets with their advertising muscle. It's not likely the media would run a negative story on a brand that is spending millions of dollars advertising with them every year. Now anyone with a computer and an Internet connection can build a blog, have a Twitter and Facebook account, and create their own media. Large companies now have less control over PR; therefore manipulative techniques once carried out are no longer so successful. Where they once controlled the environment like a cult leader, they now compete with external influences. In this day and age of open communication, PR strategies need to build on genuine credibility, and the goodwill in the community they operate within. It's good news for the SA, who understands the importance of relationships.

Business PR tactics now focus on professionalism and ethics. We are living in an era where social responsibility plays a huge role in many consumers decision-making process. Chest beating is out, and building a positive reputation and relationship with the public is in. This is why the SA can outmanoeuvre the big players and build a valuable niche.

The new breed of PR is growing fast. Online strategies such as blogs and social media have destroyed old school PR. The landscape has changed. Large corporations may employ old school PR specialists to construct and defend their reputation, however the battleground is now online for all to see.

Community

Social media has transformed the way many people build relationships. Ideally you will use social media to attract people to your website. Why? Because you control your own website. You control the messages. You control what is shared and your competitors are not there distracting your prospects. If you concentrate solely on social media to build community, the social media platform calls all the shots. They can change the rules as they please and there is nothing you can do about it. I've seen it before – where someone could build a large list and publish content that would reach all of them. Then the social media platform limits the percentage of how many recieve the content… unless you pay, of course! I've seen people invest thousands of dollars building a social media following, only to see the rules change and the rug pulled from under their feet. Focus on your own website and build your community around it: then you call the shots!

Social Proof - Swimming with the Sharks

If you want to make social work, let me cut to the chase, social proof is what people are looking for online prior to making a purchase. You may say you are a great business with a great product or service, but why should anyone believe you?

Customers purchase from businesses that have happy customers who share their success stories. What customers say about your business is worth more than anything you say about yourself. Create a customer-centric experience in your business worth raving about. Small details matter. Excellent businesses answer the phone politely and address your questions promptly. When you make an appointment and arrive at the building you are greeted with a smile. During your meeting you are given full attention. Sounds simple? Ensuring you do the basics well, helps you get excellent testimonials and word-of-mouth. Word-of-mouth is the simplest, most cost effective marketing system there is.

Poor companies don't answer their phone, so you leave a message. A few days later someone calls you back and asks why you called. You make an appointment. You arrive and find the office is a mess, you aren't sure where to sit, or if you even want to. They keep you waiting and when they finally arrive, the employee working with you accepts phone calls and text messages. Be honest with yourself, does this sound like your business in any way?

Get the groundwork done right. Provide a fantastic experience for customers so they speak well of your business and want to help you.

Then, politely asking for testimonials or feedback for case studies should be a breeze. Get it wrong and it can be a disaster, eating away at your business and making what should be simple, complicated.

With social media tools now at our figure-tips, good word-of-mouth has the power to be spread far and wide, fast. The problem is negative word-of-mouth tends to spread further, faster. Unfortunately many people love a good whinge. The customer experience you create has never been more important since every man and his dog is now a publisher online through social media.

There are a lot of sharks online these days. You can't be sure who is a legitimate business and who is not. I'm sure we have all visited websites that looked professional, only to discover they are not quite what they said they were. Overcome scepticism by building credibility through social proof. One of the most powerful, easy ways to do this is through testimonials. Video testimonials are ideal since they can't easily be fabricated like a written testimonial. If you see a real person explaining their experience, it's much more believable. It doesn't need to be an expensive process. A simple digital video across a boardroom table may be all you need, and it tends to appear far more genuine that way. If you don't have the time, or find it hard to get people in front of a camera, written testimonials are still good. Try to get a photo so people can identify with a real person, and include as much personal, relevant info as you can. For example, the full name, where they are from, their age or anything else that may be relevant to your customers. Anything people may relate to and engage with.

Happy faces of real people accompanying truthful testimonials are more effective than the polished look of stock images. They humanise your marketing, thus making it more welcoming. Also consider using photography of yourself and your team. I know, many of us are not comfortable using images of ourselves. Get over it. Your prospective customers want to see you and know who you are. Show them your authentic personality.

Case studies can turn your business successes into a magnet, drawing new customers to you. Case studies provide social proof that showcases the value of your products and services to specific types of customers. If a prospect can see how someone like them worked with you and had a great experience, they will begin to see how your business can also help them. Think back to the story about Margaret at the bank and Lisa's pitch. How can you use a story like this online?

Here are some tips for making powerful case studies that will create a lasting impression on your prospects. If you can engage people emotionally, you will be on a winner.

- Share a challenging situation your customer faced and what it meant to them emotionally. How did it affect their wellbeing? Did it have a negative impact of their personal life? Maybe their family suffered?

- Set the scene emotionally and contrast these emotions with what they experienced as a result of working with you. How did it improve their wellbeing? Was their lifestyle improved? Did they get more time or money? If so, how did they use it? Did it help them realise a dream? What did that mean to them? How did it make them feel?

Swimming Against the Stream

There's a lot of buzz around online marketing strategies and for good reason – they can be effective and low cost. However, there are many offline opportunities that are often overlooked. This chapter is about getting the right combination of online and offline marketing that works best for your business.

When you hear of new fandangle marketing strategies, don't just do it! Think differently, do it differently. Think like an SA. While everyone is pouring more money into online marketing these days, what old-school techniques can you re-use or re-invent to get your message across? It is fun to swim against the stream, and it's much easier to get noticed when you do something few others try. Direct response mail can certainly be one of those strategies.

Direct response mail still works, although these days it's much more likely to direct recipients online, rather than to a bricks-and-mortar store, or the phone. Even young people, who many assume will show no interest in direct response mail, admit to having bought something after receiving some marketing in the mail. It is interruption marketing and it still works, no matter what some of the marketing gurus are spruiking these days.

> *The opposite for courage is not cowardice, it is conformity. Even a dead fish can go with the flow.*
> **– Jim Hightower**

It's time to get tactile. While the Internet is powerful in delivering vision and sound, it's incapable of communicating through our other senses. There's still something special about getting something physical in the mail. When you see a postcard in the mail, you may relate it to getting lovely postcards from your grandmother on one of her overseas tours. That's certainly my experience. What a Vagabond she was! A handwritten note instead of a Facebook update will stand out in this digital age.

Unlike online media, that's there one second and gone the next, printed material can hang around for a while if it's done well and not dumped straight into the bin. You may have a little longer than you would online to get your message across. Similar to online marketing, you must have a strong call-to-action. There could be a time-limited special offer or some kind of coupon code in your direct response mail. SAs do this but they also believe in 'selling' their values. To sell their 'reasons'. To sell their 'why'. To sell their 'standpoint'. It's what motivates them as a business, and it also motivates their customers to respond.

Why should they buy what you are offering? What's in it for them? What are the benefits? Why is it important? It doesn't need to be lengthy. It needs to be clear, sharp, and to the point. Clarity is what counts. Once you have won them over, you'll have a far easier job of getting them to respond to your call-to-action. A time limited, special offer code or coupon creates a good reason to respond fast.

Targeting

Direct response mail is an easy way to target a specific niche. With inbound marketing you are dependent on attracting the right kinds of people. Some will be, some won't. I'm not speaking about sending mail to the general public as is the case of mass marketing either. With direct response mail, you decide who to target. You decide who you send your mail to.

Because SAs clearly understand their niche, they can more easily maximise their results while mainstream businesses often struggle. Your niche may be people who have displayed a specific set of purchasing behaviours or share a common set of interests, and so on. This form of marketing is audience-focused. It is aimed at providing a solution to a problem, or meeting a need or desire they may have.

Direct response mail is a great platform for experimental re-working. It tends to have a high conversion rate when done well and the beauty is you can scale it up and down as required. Once you know a piece works, you can send it to more people to increase your customer base, or stop it if you're already running your business at capacity. You can also re-think and re-work the piece to use for online marketing. Instinctively, you'll probably have ideas on how your piece can be adapted for online, and you can then test your ideas to see what works best. Drop what doesn't work, or tinker with it to improve the results. Don't be afraid to take it in a completely new direction.

Connecting offline with online

The Internet is a great place to expand a business, but it can also be highly competitive. If you want to achieve greater success with your marketing, consider some of the good old faithful tricks of the marketing trade to ensure you stay ahead of the crowd.

While direct response mail might be a traditional, old school form of marketing, it is by no means a thing of the past. In fact, switched on marketers are taking advantage of direct response mail for a relatively new purpose, to drive traffic to their websites. Make your website an online sales hub where you draw all your prospects through online and offline marketing techniques. From here you can more easily build the relationships and make sales.

> *"Others have seen what is and asked why. I have seen what could be and asked why not."*
> **– Pablo Picasso**

If you do choose to connect your off- and online campaigns, follow the theme through. Use the same style for your direct response mail and landing page. If the look and feel of your landing page is at odds with the direct response mail, it will confuse customers. Visitors must know immediately that they have come to the right place. The message should also follow the theme. It may expand upon or enhance what was in the printed material, or it could simply reinforce the same message in a succinct way. You don't need to sell them all over again, and you don't want them to jump through hoops. Don't lose them with complexity.

You can choose exactly who you want to target and push your message to them via direct response mail. You can't be so precise with many other marketing methods. It's a great way to reach potential customers and develop a relationship with existing customers who may have become inactive. While, due to SPAM laws, you can't shoot out thousands of emails to anyone you please, you can send good old fashioned snail-mail. Think of all those Posties you will be keeping in a job. Unlike email that is quickly and easily deleted, mail requires effort to physically engage with and open. It might be opened above the bin, but at least it's not as fast as a rapid-fire delete button in someone's email inbox.

Databases

Here's the boring bit about direct response mail, so stick with me... or get someone from your team to read this. For direct response mail, you will need a database. The database can be purchased if you are looking for brand new customers, or extracted out of software if you are approaching old customers. If you have a CRM (Customer Relationship Manager) that's gold, but you can also get data from your accounting software, project management software, computers' address book, or a Rolodex (apparently they still exist).

Your printer can let you know what format they need your database and files in. They will probably want your data in a spreadsheet so they can easily mail merge the addresses and other variable data. Hopefully you have your data in a format that you can easily convert. If it's the old Rolodex or some other non-digital format, it's probably something you want to get someone else to do.

You can do some crazy, cool things with variable data printing these days. It's not just about text but variable images based on characteristics of who you are targeting. For example, if you know Jimmy bought a blue widget last time, the direct response mail piece may show a photo for the updated and upgraded widget, also in blue since we know Jimmy likes blue.

Of course you may also build a database by having people 'opt-in' on your website. That's great for online marketing, but you probably won't have the mailing address details for this database unless you have purpose built it for this reason. Remember I suggested you ask for the minimum amount of information to increase your opt-in rate so, from that perspective, you probably wouldn't ask for an address. The flipside is, if there is a good reason for your prospects to give address details, for example, you're mailing out a free book that requires an address, then you will increase your chances of success. Remember, the SA knows it's good to give away something of percieved value. This is a time when this approach can work wonders.

When you create your database, ideally you'll use it more than once, hopefully many times. You can experiment with different offers in different formats and see what gets the best response. How often you send information will depend on your business and industry. What kind of information you send, and what design best communicates your intended message, will also require experimentation.

Direct response mail can get your message out to a large group of prospects fast. It can produce rapid results, so it is easy to see if it's working. For example, if a company sends 10,000 direct response mail letters, and 1,000 prospects responded to the promotion, resulting in 100 sales, the business owner can quickly see how well it worked and decide to send it to 100,000 more people knowing that will probably create 1,000 sales. It's not rocket-science. The other option is to tinker with it a little first and try sending it to another 10,000. You can then work out what converted best and scale that up. You won't get this luxury by advertising in your local phone book, or using SEO.

Personalisation

I already mentioned variable data briefly, personalising your direct response mail increases conversion rates. Digital printing techniques have made this easier and more cost effective than it was in the past. Direct response mail generally works better when it is made as unique as possible and you have taken the time to address customers personally. There are a variety of techniques to experiment with. Some marketers recommend handwritten envelopes, some include a small freebie so it's bulky or lumpy mail. You'll need to consider the costs and benefits before you adopt any of these options, but they are worth experimenting with. Look for high perceived value and low cost.

Some great reasons to use physical mail and not only email:

- Studies have shown that **direct response mail is one of the most profitable**, cost effective ways of targeting your ideal prospects with a specific message.

- Direct response mail **provides a way to communicate with past**

customers about your new special offers such as time-limited offers and new product launches.

- It can be difficult to get your customers back to your website at times. With direct response mail delivered to their letterbox, **you are more likely to get noticed**. It's interruption marketing at its best.

- Physically sending mail to your target market **can help you create solid connections**. For example, you could send a sample of your product, or some other physical item, to help you get noticed. You don't have that tactile advantage online.

- **Responses can be easily tracked**, making this form of marketing measurable. This also allows you to determine what works best, experiment and refine your efforts.

Call-to-Action

There's more to successful direct response mailing than great copy and eye-catching graphic design. For many, creating the concept and content for a direct response campaign can become an overwhelming, complicated tasks. It's easy to get caught up in the process, however if you focus on the call-to-action you are half way there.

Both the content and design should be used to highlight one central call-to-action per mailing. Keep it simple, useful, and make it obvious how to take action. The design should be simple too. It's not about winning design awards, it's about generating a response.

Direct response mail requires a compelling offer that provides a strong reason for your target audience to respond, which in this case could be to visit your website. You could try motivating your target market with a free offer, discount coupons, or a chance to win something if they respond now.

Always use urgency in your offer. If people feel they could miss out, the perceived value of your offer increases. Think back to the lessons learnt from cult-leaders. You could create urgency by appealing to people's emotions. When there is urgency, your target market will be motivated to act on your offer immediately. Be clear with your urgency and place it near your call-to-action. Make a special offer within a specific timeframe that people can respond to easily.

The ultimate goal of a marketing campaign is to persuade people to buy (even if that means buying into an idea, and not spending money), but initially the desired action might be to entice people to take the first step. You may want them to visit your landing page to order a free information product. This could be a free report, short e-book, samples to try, or a free webinar. Much of the writing strategies unpacked in the Content Marketing chapter apply when writing for direct response mail too. The main difference is you need to be ultra clear on your call-to-action and can afford to make your content more 'salesy'. Direct marketing content will be less about educating and more about persuading your readers, so it should be benefits-focused. You headline needs to be engaging and interesting, encouraging your recipients to read on, and your call-to-action needs to be the real kicker. It needs to be an irresistible offer. Start with your call-to-action and work back from there. Use social proof such as testimonials from satisfied customers. Identify your key message and ensure it is written in a way that appeals to your recipients. The better you define your niche and tailor your message accordingly, the more likely you are to see a strong response.

Follow up

It's a busy world where we are all bombarded with information and sometimes it can be difficult to be heard. Sending something in the mail direct to a prospect is a great way to get your message out there.

Consider sending more than one piece of direct response mail. Typically there's a far better response if you follow it up. How many times you mail out during a particular marketing campaign depends on your budget and your own comfort levels. I've found myself on some mailing lists, and while I liked the company and their offer at first, they sent so much stuff it frustrated me and I've decided not to get involved with them, even though I love their products.

If you are following up, ideally follow up with the same offer or a slightly improved version that is presented in a slightly different way. There will be people who intended on responding to your initial offer but became distracted, and those that didn't engage with the first piece who may do so when it's presented differently. There will be others who didn't even see the first piece. Their partner may have opened the mail for them and binned it on their behalf (naughty partner). Mix it up; if you started with a letter, you could follow up with a postcard. Think outside the box and surprise them. Be an SA!

Experiment, test, and measure. Create two variations, A and B, of your direct response mail, testing small differences. For example, you could changes the headline or the design slightly. Send A to 50% of your list, and B to the remaining 50%. Track the response rate so you can improve your results incrementally over time. An easy way to do it is to create two different landing page URL's, sending letter A recipients to one and letter B to the other. That way you will quickly see which letter attracted the greatest number of people, because it's easy to add basic analytics on a website to track this for you. Track how many completed your call-to-action online, and assess the results. You can go through the A/B testing process multiple times until you are satisfied with the results. Once you have great results, you can scale up your efforts sending your campaigns to a larger list and you can be reasonably confident what results to expect. Remember it's about perfecting not perfection. There's always something that could be improved but at some stage you have got to pull the pin and go for it.

Mass marketing

Often, the cost to print direct response mail is much less than other printed marketing material because you only produce the required quantity, according to the size of your database. Mass marketing via letterbox drops produces excessive waste, although it's effective in targeting geographic regions rather than specific people and you don't have postage costs. Letterbox drops are cheap if the deliverer doesn't dump them under the bridge. The value and costs will depend on the nature of your business and what produces the best results for you. It's similar to comparing emails with physical letters. While email marketing is less expensive than printed material, the response rates are often significantly less. It is a numbers game.

We can't ignore the environmental costs either. For some businesses it will be obvious, printed direct response mail or letterbox drops are not suitable. For others you may know instinctively it may not be suitable, or you may not be comfortable doing it. If you choose not to use printed material for whatever reason, that's great. Remember, this book is not a one-size-fits-all system. It's up to you to pick and choose what you want to apply, and even reject. That's all part of being an SA.

Collaboration Learnt the Hard Way

To be a successful SA, you have to be agile, responding to opportunities as they come up. Make a decision to reduce what you do and outsource to specialists who have the gifts and talents to do the job quicker and better than you can.

Collaboration can help you overcome overwhelming situations when done well. If it's done poorly it can have the opposite effect. Don't try to do everything yourself since it's a poor use of your time. Learn to rely on others for their specialist skills or to complete mundane, time-consuming tasks. Most businesses need a team, whether that be employees or external support from specialists or virtual assistants.

If you look online, the amount of resources available are countless. This creates the illusion that all the information you ever need is there for you to do it yourself. Don't be lured into this trap. Even with all the information in the world, it doesn't make you skilled enough to carry out every task, nor should you want to. I can buy fantastic cook-books by the best chefs in the world. They can tell me exactly what I need to do and when I need to do it, but I'm still going to suck at cooking. At best, I'll follow the recipe and end up with a nice result, but it's never going to be as good as the chef who created the recipe. Seek help on areas you are not familiar with, not good at, or don't like doing, so you can be freed up to do what you do best.

Over the years I've learnt a lot working with people in various community groups and business networking organisations. These groups give you an opportunity to collaborate with people you normally wouldn't mix with and those that have a different standpoint. Being a Christian, it's been a fantastic experience working along-side people from different faiths and different beliefs, to work towards common goals. I've particularly enjoyed working with a Muslim friend who does a lot of work for the needy, particularly orphans and youth. While we don't agree on a number of issues, there are things we do agree on and we work together in a way that I find refreshing. I also enjoy being able to better understand different perspectives. There is much to learn in times where we don't agree and relationships are strained.

Much of what I have learnt working with people I learnt the hard way in times of strained relationships. Let's pick up the story from the chapter "What's at your Centre" when my son, Max, was born. It was a life changing time where I needed to re-think my business. I had been very busy with work, but now had other priorities that deserved my time. Now I was a father.

I was still quite new in business and doing well working solo, but I knew that I had come to the point where I couldn't do all the work on my own and do justice to Max or Lisa. By this time, Lisa was pregnant again with another son due 19 months after Max. I realised I needed someone to support me by doing some of the work that was on my plate. At that time the logical choice for me was to employ a full time graphic designer, since much of the work I was doing involved graphic design at the time. I started looking for a junior full-time graphic designer as that's what I could afford. They could do the basic design requirements while I focussed on the high-end design, project management, and clients. A friend of mine, Anna, had recently finished her design course and put her hand up for the job. While her work wasn't all that great, I convinced myself it would be best to hire her since she was a friend and would have my best interests at heart. Not only that, we had similar interests and were involved in community groups together. These connections meant she would be dependable and someone I could trust – or so I thought.

I had many fears employing someone and knowing she was a friend put my mind at ease. Decisions based on fear are often bad ideas and this one proved to be one of my worst. At first things went well. The design work wasn't great, but it was serviceable and I could fix things fairly quickly. She was a junior after all and that was to be expected. Together we were getting more work done than I could ever do on my own and life was good. Over the months, I noticed the work getting done was tapering off. It seemed Anna's enthusiasm for the job was dropping fast, and I had no idea what to do about it. Tasks were not being completed accurately, and the speed at which they were being done was insufficient to a point where some jobs cost me more to pay her to complete than what I was making from that job.

> *"Politeness is the poison of collaboration."*
> **– Edwin Land**

I thought maybe she just needed to be refreshed so she could think creatively and work productively, so I gave her additional breaks every day to go for a walk. That didn't seem to help. I sent her away from work early so she could go and help with the community group activities we were involved with, while I stayed behind and finished projects she was working on. I convinced myself this was a good idea since it was my way of contributing to the group while potentially re-energising her. There was still no positive response. I had no idea what to try next and I had a big challenge approaching.

Lisa was pregnant with our second baby and I had planned to take some time off and leave the projects for Anna to manage. It was a scary time for me. Every project was dependent on me up until this time and now I was going to suddenly step back and have to rely on Anna who seemed to be increasingly disinterested. Again I convinced myself she would do the right thing by me since we were friends. How wrong I was.

The Simple Manifesto

The day of the birth of my second son, Charlie, came while we were on deadline for a couple of projects. I had a mini-breakdown driving home, not knowing exactly what to do. I was fearful of what might happen to my work and angry at myself for not focussing on the family at this time. The birth went well and we were delighted. He was a big, healthy baby (5 .1kg) we named Charlie.

The following morning I called Anna while driving back to the hospital to check in and see how everything was going. I told her which project was most urgent and to complete that before moving on to the next priority, even if other clients put pressure on her. I told her if clients put pressure on her, she could direct them to call me on my mobile phone and I would take care of it. She agreed and my mind was at ease thinking it was all taken care of.

Some clients were going to get work done a little later than usual, but I believed they would understand, given the birth of my son and the fact we were a micro-business.

That proved to be true; our clients were completely understanding of the situation and happy for us. One graciously called me and told me to forget about his project for the moment and focus on the baby. I had spent time investing into client relationships so making a little withdrawal at this time was completely fine.

The following day I phoned Anna to check the progress, only to find out the urgent job had not been done. It would have only taken an hour of two and Anna could have then moved on to other projects. Another client had asked Anna to complete their job immediately and she went ahead and did that, despite agreeing with me otherwise. There and then I knew the wheels were falling off and I had to re-think the business. I felt like I just needed to keep Anna happy for the next week or two so she would get some work done. She wanted to work from home, which made sense since she was working alone anyway, and I agreed. She then decided I would need to pay her mobile phone bill since she would need to use it working from home. I reluctantly agreed, just wanting to keep her happy.

We were running online project management software to track time spent on projects for billing purposes. A few days later I checked in to see how things were going, so I didn't need to bother Anna on the phone. I had other projects to give her, but just wanted her to finish what was on her plate first so she didn't become overwhelmed. What a shocking surprise when I found Anna had entered time to go to the local shopping centre to recharge her phone, not once but twice, for a total of over two hours for a round trip that could be done in under 20 minutes.

Simple tasks in the system were not being done. I checked in later and found she had entered a trip to visit a client for a few hours. Apparently the client wanted to 'catch up'. Anna had never, ever been out to a meeting, and travelling so far for a vague meeting would never be warranted. Later I found out the client had propositioned Anna to work with her directly. I guess he was thinking he would arrange a cheaper deal while I was away. The meeting was for the purpose of poaching my client, and she had the audacity to take hours off her work-day while I was paying her to do it. It was heart breaking.

In this desperate, stressful time I decided to quickly restructure my business. I needed to re-organise what was at the centre of the business and simplify it. I decided to change how I worked with my biggest client who was consuming the most time, yet producing the lowest dollar value per hour for work done. I proposed a higher fee knowing this would probably mean we lost them as a client. They told me they would hire a full-time designer instead. I called a meeting with Anna, let her know we would be no longer working for our large client and therefore didn't have enough work for her either. I told her she could apply for the full-time role with my ex-client if she wished, which she

"A successful man is one who can lay a firm foundation with the bricks others have thrown at him."
– David Brinkley

did, and got the job. My conscience was clear – I had done the best thing for everyone concerned.

In a time when I should have been enjoying my new-born son, I had hit an all-time low. Someone who I had considered a friend had pulled the rug from beneath my feet. Anna's father was the Senior Executive of the community group we were a part of. We were good friends up until this point, but it's fair to say the relationship was strained and never recovered. The Senior Executive took every opportunity to wrongly accuse me of anything he could and made life difficult. This may have been subconscious but was certainly out of anger directed at me. I kept my nose clean and didn't involve anyone else in the debate, but it came to a point where I'd had enough. I met the Executive at a local coffee shop and I called him on his regular, repeated accusations. He stormed out of the meeting: What I had said was undeniable, and it was clear we could no longer be a part of the community group we had invested so much of our time, energy, and resources into. I called Lisa to tell her what had happened. The Executive re-shaped all of this into a different story to his leadership team. We never tried to defend ourselves publicly, we just moved on, heartbroken and desperate. It took time to get over how much this hurt, yet the lessons learnt at this time in my life became instrumental in the way I re-thought, re-built and re-positioned my business from that point on. That re-thinking led to this book.

Shrinking for Simple Growth

There are a number of reasons why the traditional business model of employing staff doesn't work for small business and entrepreneurs. Employing full-timers is often out of reach for small businesses since they don't have the quantity of work to warrant it. In these cases, sometimes businesses broaden the scope of work they require to make up full-time hours for a new employee. Employing one person will always mean hiring a limited skillset. While it's fine to batch a range of low-end tasks to one person, trying to get a highly experienced, qualified, specialist team member to do something outside their core skillset is dangerous. Beware of this approach! You are likely to scrape the bottom of the barrel in terms of the quality of workers who will be prepared to do this kind of work. The other traditional option is to employ a part-timer. This can work, however you reduce the pool of talent to those interested in part-time. They probably have other areas in their life that require their dedication and focus. The set up costs can also be significant, since a part-timer will usually need just as many resources as a full-time staff member. Consider the computer and software requirements, and basic requirements like desk, office chair, and even the space required for the new part-time team member.

In years gone by, the majority of the western world would study to get the best possible career in their chosen field. It was a lifelong decision. The dream was to be employed in a large, successful corporation, and work for promotions to advance their position. The more successful a corporation was, the more people they would employ, and the more secure an employee's role. Growing the business by increasing the number of employees was the norm.

The world has changed. With the advancement of technology, new models of business have emerged. Growth by large corporations and small business alike are not dependent on the size of the team you employ. Welcome to the world of outsourcing to specialists. The new breed of professionals no longer seek to establish themselves permanently with one employer. At least, the best professionals you could work with don't think this way. They seek to establish themselves as a specialist in their field. They often have a range of projects on the go for different clients, or work from project to project for various businesses.

There is a growing trend of companies downsizing these days. It's not always because they are struggling. It's not always for 'cheaper' offshore labour either. Often it's the attraction of a more flexible workforce with specialist skills that entices businesses to downsize.

Most small businesses have fluctuating needs at various levels. Businesses find their requirements can vary from week to week. Downsizing and outsourcing also enables you to streamline your systems and processes. For example, if you sell a product online, you might have the wholesaler ship it out on your behalf, rather that rent a warehouse, hire staff and have all the complications that can be caused by this traditional, complex business model.

You don't need offices or full-time staff. Who wants to waste time and energy managing and motivating staff? Outsourcing partners are self-motivated because they understand the quality of their work will lead to ongoing work and referrals. When I say outsourcing, I'm not just talking about offshore providers either. There are huge advantages to outsourcing to other local professionals in your area. The specialists you need can be working right in your backyard, and collaboration grows both your businesses.

With this new model of business, you can work from home or a co-working facility with others. I personally chose to work in a co-working, shared office space Lisa and I own so I can separate work and personal life a little. It helps me clear my head, but everyone's preferences are different. I find it easier to focus at work, particularly with young kids at home who want to play all day. I also understand the advantages of working from home. It's got to be a good thing to be able to work in your boxer shorts all day. It helps if you remember to put a shirt on if you have a Skype meeting scheduled, or nip out to the coffee shop.

Selecting independent contractors for your team can be difficult, particularly when the project is technical with much of the work happening behind the scenes. When you approach a potential team member, actively listen to them and prompt them for their advice and suggestions. Although you have a goal in mind, you may not know the best way to achieve it. Hire people who will consult with you, ask questions, and make recommendations. After listening to your needs, a good potential team member will explain to you what they believe to be the best solution, or provide options highlighting any pros and cons to consider. Good team players will keep you in the loop throughout the project. They will also make you aware of any modifications needed during the process.

Avoid outsourcing to large organisation who use Account Managers.

Work directly with hands-on people. People who have technical know-how and experience are more likely to be able to help you in a collaborative, team-like manner.

Select team members who will make the process as simple as possible for you. They should be professional yet affordable, and someone you can trust. Hire people who are strong in the areas of your

"In order to pick something up, you've got to put something down."
– Todd Stocker

weakness. Because our world has become so fast-paced, team members may sometimes speed through their tasks without understanding your goals and expectations. As the leader of your business, your primary responsibility is the big picture. You do not want to micro-manage projects. Hire people with a good eye for detail. Hire people who will keep your project on time and on brief. People with attention to detail ask questions, provide suggestions, and seek clarification. Don't let them bore you with technical jargon, trying to impress you. Cut to the chase and ask them, how their recommendations will produce a better outcome for your business.

While you may have a great deal of knowledge about your business, assume your new team member knows nothing about your industry, and even less about your business. Provide them with as much information as possible. If you have a limited budget, tell them up front. They may be able to make more appropriate suggestions if they understand your limitations. Total honesty and transparency will allow your team to come up with the most appropriate solution for your situation. They may be able to recommend smaller, more achievable steps to accommodate your requirements.

A common mistake many businesses make is to continually shop around looking for a better deal. For example, they may select one provider to design a website, another to provide SEO, another to handle advertising, and still another to host the website. While you could save a few bucks shopping around for the 'best' deal in each category, it will cost your time. Consider the time taken to find and manage a mixed team like this. What happens when something goes wrong? The web designer blames the host, the host blames the SEO company, and the SEO company blames the designer. When possible, it is far better to have one supplier for a set of tasks. When you have team members accountable for specific requirements in your business, you will build a stronger, more collaborative working relationship. They will feel empowered by the tasks you have entrusted to them.

If one person is capable of handling a few related tasks you will minimise the time it takes managing them, and maximise efficiencies; but that is not always possible. Virtual Assistants are a good example of this, they tend to do a range of low-end, admin-related tasks, freeing up your time to concentrate on the success of your business.

Most businesses, particularly small businesses and start-up companies, have limited budgets so the temptation can be to hire a Virtual Assistant to do a broad range of tasks that require specialist knowledge. It's a bad idea to have the same person who does your bookkeeping also run your marketing campaigns. Some areas of your business require specialist knowledge.

An outsourced team member is likely to thank you for sending more work while a traditional employee is likely to complain they are overworked. They understand the more they can help you, the more you will use their services, and potentially give them referrals if you don't have them booked solid already. It's in their best interest to give you a high quality service; the level of service that builds confidence for a long-term working relationship. It is unlikely a traditional employee will equal this level of motivation.

Sadly, when building a team of any kind there will be personality clashes from time to time. When your team is made up of people you outsource to who are leaders in their own specific industries, it raises its own set of challenges. They may be head-strong and often have different opinions on how they can best achieve the desired result.

Who should be in charge? Whose opinion is most important? Yours of course! However it's helpful to understand other opinions may be equally valid. Differing opinions and insights can be challenging, but also enlightening when everyone feels heard. Welcome discussions so challenges can be addressed and clarity established.

Here's a classic example of personalities that can clash:

Graphic Designers v Web Programmers

Designers are often focused on making projects visually attractive and appealing to potential customers. They complete projects with an artistic mindset and are always striving to create the most aesthetically pleasing combination of colour, fonts, and graphic elements. They love to play with various styles, always looking for the next great trend in design. This is all useful.

On the other hand, web programmers, often have goals that are centred on functionality and accessibility for website users. Their thinking tends to be more functional and technical, focusing on what will make the project the most efficient and practical. They are masters of code, and are subject to the limitations it imposes.

So who should be in charge? Who is more important to the project? The answer is they are both equally valuable, and both need to have input into a website project. The truth is, when developing a website you need both sides of the spectrum. You need to balance creative and analytical thinking. This is a scenario I deal with in my line of work. You will find similar scenarios across a range of functions within your own business. Building a culture of collaboration improves communication and minimises the damage when differing opinions do get a little heated.

When it comes to websites, many developers are torn between aesthetics and functionality, and few are capable of delivering both. When you are designing a website you don't have to choose between looking good or working well. Accomplishing both is always achievable, if you pick the right team and the right blend of skills.

The SAs Dream Team

As an SA, it is likely your team will expand and contract as needs change. Your success will depend largely on the knowledge and the skills of the team members you select. When making your decision, there are a number of attributes to consider.

If you meet in person, how do they present themselves? How do they present themselves online in social media? Do they conduct themselves in a professional and courteous manner? Pay attention to small details and your gut feelings. They don't need to look like they walked straight out of a major corporation or straight off the cat-walk, however there may be visual clues that highlight aspects of their lives and work that may be of concern.

While presentation can be misleading at times, it does provide some clues about the character and attitude of the person. If they dress like a 'rock star', they may be showing you something about their approach to life and work. Their attitude may enhance or hinder your team. How will this kind of person deal with your requirements? How will they deal with deadlines or pressure?

Good communication skills are a huge key to building your dream team. After all, collaboration is dependent on great communication. This is a big part of why outsourcing locally is often best. Communicating with people in a different time zone, whose native language is not the same as yours can be incredibly challenging and time consuming.

Mutual respect for all team members working together is important. Although the specialist you are looking to hire does not need to have skills outside his or her area of expertise, they do need to respect and value people with different skillsets and perspectives. If you have an arrogant team member who does not respect people they perceive to be less important in your team, then collaboration will be a constant struggle. As the business leader, you need to set the example and demonstrate respect for everyone. Some team members naturally feel intimidated by the 'boss', so create a platform where you express your respect for them. A little praise goes a long way! Feeling valued will encourage them to have creative input into your projects. Chances are they have experiences with projects similar to yours and have seen other approaches that you may not have considered. Team members who work outside your business premises often think more creatively than in-house employees. They have a different standpoint. Make the most of this insight; remember that an SA is always ready to learn.

Check the history of a potential team member. Do they have glowing testimonials from past clients? Are you able to conduct reference checks on them? Do they have a portfolio or some other way to demonstrate their past projects and work experiences? It's common for people to exaggerate their involvement in past projects. They may have done 1% of the project but make it sound like they did much more. Quiz them a little to get some bearings on what they actually did. If they were referred to you by someone you trust, that's ideal, but not always possible.

You may not personally like a team member you bring on board. They wouldn't be someone you would want to hang out with on the weekend. As long as they are not going to upset the harmony of your team, that's fine! SAs focus on how well the person can fulfil a role and save them time. Being likeable helps. However, don't discriminate against someone for personality. Look at how well they can fulfil the goals and objectives within your team, and think about how they can help you focus on your core business.

Choosing a team member should be a carefully considered business decision, even if the project is small and temporary. You may have a specific short-term need that is front of mind but you should consider the time it takes having to explain requirements to a new team member. If you can batch low-end tasks and have one person handle them all, you will save yourself hours. Consider the time wasted with pleasantries, basic explanations of the business, and introductions to other team members. It's all costly to the SA, so think long term. Having a clearly defined standpoint will enable you to quickly communicate why you do business the way you do. If they can buy into that idea, or at least appreciate it, they will collaborate with you more effectively.

Always remember, there are almost always many other potential team members capable of your project requirements. If it's not working out, move on quickly. Fire fast. I should have done this with Anna! On the flip side, when you find a good team member, hold onto them. Over time, you will find you need to invest less time into them explaining your requirements. They will be working from a base of knowledge, so explaining new projects becomes easier. Your time spent with team members becomes an investment not an expense when you use them repeatedly for new projects.

It's not hard finding new team members. 'Google' it and you'll probably find a whole range of providers in your local area. Lean towards independent contractors or small teams of two or three people. If you work with large organisations, they will have control of how your work gets done and you will be just one of many customers. It's far better to work with one or two people who appreciate and depend upon you as a source of income.

There are a range of websites to connect you with potential team members. It can be overwhelming sifting through all the options, however most of the online systems have handy filtering systems. If you do choose to work with someone overseas, I suggest you put a high level of English as a priority in your search and selection criteria. Miscommunication and misunderstandings are the most common problems when working with someone who doesn't usually read, write, or speak the same language as you, so minimise this risk by assessing their language skills.

I've seen many business owners hire people who appeared cheap but proved to be costly. You may be able to get cheaper work done offshore, however you should consider your time investment in instructing someone overseas. If English is not their native language, be prepared to spend countless hours late at night behind a PC monitor explaining and re-explaining your requirements.

These days we communicate electronically no matter where the person is, usually by sending an email. It is generally an advantage if your team is working in the same time zone as you and understands the culture you are a part of but it's not essential. Unfortunately there are a lot of 'smoke and mirror' operators if you do choose someone on the other side of the globe. There are some people who will promise whatever they feel you need so they win your project. Remember what we learnt from the Con-Artist: Sometimes we may be mislead.

For the SA, local independent contractors and freelancers are the best bet. When outsourcing like this, the hourly rate will usually be higher than the hourly rate of a full or part time employee, however you need to consider all the costs. When you hire someone in the traditional way you pay them whether they are working or not. When the Internet is down, you pay them. When they are sick, you pay them. When they need to relieve themselves, you pay them. The truth is, you will be paying for a whole lot of stuff that is not beneficial in any way to you or your business. When using freelancers or outsourced small teams, you only pay for productivity. You only pay for the hours they worked, or the completed project you agreed on. You don't pay for office space and the costs of running that office. There are ways to negotiate lower rates too. If you have ongoing, consistent requirements you may be able to negotiate a better rate using a retainer since it's easier for your team member to predict workloads and therefore, don't have as much downtime other freelancers or small teams do.

I know I might be harping on this point, but it's important. There are two costs to always consider – time and money! Sometimes it may be wise to stretch your budget a little to get excellent service that will cost you less time reviewing and micromanaging every little task required. That way you can get on with growing your business and winning more work for everyone.

Consider the time you put into your team as an investment. You need to keep them in order to get a return on that investment. By outsourcing to regular team members, you're free to focus more on your core functions knowing your projects are in professional hands. Over time, a strong working relationship is built. Where once a detailed discussion may have been needed, your team members will soon understand your requirements. In time, you may be able to send a couple of sentences and that's all they need, because they understand you and your business. The right team member can save your sanity.

Outsourced small teams and individuals shouldn't require your personal supervision. They look after their own resources, and their personal problems don't become yours. You don't need to worry about ongoing training, it's their responsibility to update their skills and knowledge.

To make sure your projects are completed on time, on brief, and on budget, create a plan in advance. To save yourself time, discuss your goals and objectives with the relevant team member and ask for them to prepare a plan with a timeline. If they have prepared the plan, it's difficult to make excuses for not meeting its requirements. Of course, you may need to review the plan with the team members, but you may be pleasantly surprised by the commitments they make by preparing their own plan.

Clumsy Corporates

Large corporations become bogged down with policy and procedure manuals, style guides and endless documentations in the hope of producing consistent results. I've worked on design style guides for massive corporations over the years and I avoid that kind of work now. Why? Because they almost always add layers of complexity that inhibit creativity, slow projects down, and are rarely followed exactly anyway. They become overwhelming. They often become out-dated soon after being published, making them even more confusing. All of these attributes are the enemy of SAs. The end goal for these documents is to create consistency, and large corporations don't have many alternatives.

When building your team to collaborate with, share your unique standpoint. This becomes your guide to creating consistency, not some hard and fast set of rules. Your position provides direction on every situation. In the early stages, a new team member needs to have guidance and feedback since they may interpret details differently to you. As the working relationship develops, you'll find less input is required from you as they pick up the heart of what's important in your business. Encourage your team to be creative while remaining aligned with your vision. If your team members are all local, arrange face-to-face brainstorming sessions from time to time. If they are scattered around the globe, find ways to connect with them online so they have a sense of human interaction and being involved in something bigger than themselves.

> *"The problem with the rat race is that even if you win, you're still a rat."*
>
> **– Lily Tomlin**

The Power of Small

SAs starting new projects or ventures learn, and continue to experiment, by testing, measuring, and improving them over time. As they learn what works and what doesn't, they adapt. Not every new business project makes it. In fact many don't survive the first year, so it's ideal to test your ideas with a minimal investment of time or money.

Keep your team relatively small. Today you can outsource almost any project you can think of. If you continually hunt for a cheaper deal, you will find yourself in a real mess with files all over the place and tasks half done. For this reason, keep only a small group of people around you who you can trust. These are the people who will do the core work.

Outsourcing to freelancers or small teams is the perfect solution for small, dynamic businesses. They work from their own premises, use their own equipment, and cover their own expenses. This new breed of professionals run fully fledged operations, and have the tools and skills necessary to work remotely.

Once a strong working relationship is established, you can set them up with an email address associated with your business so any correspondence they send relevant to your business works seamlessly with your usual business practices. This can help all your team members feel like they belong.

For my latest recommendations on outsourcing and collaboration, visit www.simplemanifesto.com/members

The Simple Manifesto 2.0

We have come a full circle in many ways throughout this book, a spiral if you will. While doing more and adding complexity to your business will ensure it spirals out of control on a downward trajectory, The Simple Manifesto is created to help you get your business and life on an upward spiral by simplifying your approach to business. Remember, this is not a step-by-step, one-size-fits-all book. It's about finding simple, incremental, consistent improvement with minimal time or financial investment.

I hope you find the low hanging fruit in your business as a result of this book. Those things that will give you the greatest value now, and propel you forward.

This is not the end, it's just the beginning of your journey and what shapes you from here on. I've shared lessons with you that I've learnt in my own business and life adventures. Some lessons have been painful, and some a joy, but all have been valuable for me and I hope they have been for you too.

I've shown you my own unique standpoint. I've shown you my perspective based on my own life experiences. I've shown you my nonconformist views based on my journey. I've shown you how I approached change and transformation in my own business and life, and finally, I've shown you my position.

Now it's your turn…

I'd love to hear your success stories as a result of this book. I'd also like to hear about your challenges.

Here are a few questions for you, and I really do want to hear your answers:

- What have you been challenged by in this book?

- What is your unique standpoint and how have you clarified it?

- How have you rebelled against your industry, making you the nonconformist?

- What approach have you taken in getting your business to the next level?

"I am not a genius, I am just curious. I ask many questions and when the answer is simple, then God is answering."

– Albert Einstein

- How have you established your rock-solid position in the marketplace?

- What have you chosen to implement and why?

- What may you consider implementing later and why?

- What have you chosen to reject and why?

Submit your answers at www.simplemanifesto.com/members. With your help, I will release "The Simple Manifesto 2.0" (working title) and I want your story to be a part of it. I don't know what it looks like, and I don't know what it covers, because that depends on you. I already have some stories I'd like to share with you in this next adventure. To give you a little taster, Lisa and I have had a third child, Grace. I know I said few things are perfect, but she is darn close. Anyway, there is another life changing story around the time Grace was born and I'll save that up for The Simple Manifesto 2.0, so stay tuned.

I look forward to hearing from you, the SA. Let's journey together...

(The Access Code to www.simplemanifesto.com/members is SNAP.)